FROST'S
LAWS AND BY-LAWS
OF AMERICAN SOCIETY.

A CONDENSED BUT THOROUGH TREATISE ON

ETIQUETTE AND ITS USAGES IN AMERICA.

CONTAINING PLAIN AND RELIABLE DIRECTIONS FOR

DEPORTMENT IN EVERY SITUATION IN LIFE,

ON THE FOLLOWING SUBJECTS:

Letters of Introduction.
Salutes and Salutations,
Calls,
Conversation,
Invitations,
Dinner Company,
Balls,
Morning and Evening Parties,
Visiting,
Street Etiquette,
Riding and Driving,
Travelling,
Etiquette in Church,
Etiquette for Places of Amusement,
Servants,
Hotel Etiquette,
Etiquette at Weddings,
Baptisms and Funerals,
Etiquette with Children and at the Card Table,
Visiting Cards,
Letter-Writing,
The Lady's Toilet,
The Gentleman's Toilet,

BESIDES ONE HUNDRED UNCLASSIFIED LAWS

APPLICABLE TO ALL OCCASIONS.

BY S. A. FROST.

AUTHOR OF "FROST'S LETTER-WRITER," ETC.

NEW YORK:
DICK & FITZGERALD, PUBLISHERS.

PREFACE.

For a long time the little book which we now offer to the public has been wanted in the library of the fashionable world; the customs, the etiquette, the different obligations which society imposes upon those who live in its midst, change frequently, and although the general principles are the same, although politeness and civility are of all epoques and times, nevertheless there are few persons so entirely at home in all the forms that they do not on some occasion feel hesitation as to the proper manner of conducting themselves.

Indeed, besides the broader and more essential rules of politeness, there are certain conventionalities adopted by good society, which, sanctioned by custom and absolute obligation, cannot, without some good reason, be neglected by the truly polite gentleman or lady. Every day the question is raised whether such and such a custom is adopted, received, and proper; there will constantly arise a doubt about the details of some ceremony, the proper hour for some entertainment, the true etiquette for some occasion. At such a time, there is a regret felt that there is not at hand, in one's own library, a safe guide, an experienced counsellor, who will answer such questions, so trifling in appearance, so important in reality.

A breach of etiquette, an involuntarily omission of some point of politeness, may often have a serious influence upon the future of the perpetrator. None of these little details are to be scorned; they have each and every one a value.

It is to meet the want already mentioned that this little volume has been prepared. It makes no claim to originality; but its aim is to be perfectly reliable. English, French, and American authorities of weight have been consulted, and nothing admitted that was not sanctioned by experience and the customs of the best society.

Books, it is very true, have been already written upon this subject; but they are for the most part filled with useless details, and often do not contain what is of most importance. The aim of the Editor of the present work has been to avoid both extremes, to select only what was useful, reliable, and well established, and to reject only what was valueless or mere repetition.

The subjects treated are all classed that they may have easy reference, and admit of consultation at a moment's notice.

The little book goes forth with one pretension only, one ambition alone—to be useful.

CONTENTS.

THE

LAWS AND BY-LAWS

OF AMERICAN SOCIETY.

ETIQUETTE AND ITS USES.

THERE are a great many people, in other respects perfectly estimable (which makes the complaint against them the more grievous) who maintain that the laws of nature are the only laws of binding force among the units which compose society. They do not assert their doctrine in so many words, but practically they avow it, and they are not slow to express their contempt for the "ridiculous etiquette" which is declared by their opponents to be essential to the well being of society. These people are probably a law to themselves in such matters; they obey in their rules of conduct those instincts of propriety and good manners which were implanted in them at their birth, and cultivated probably by their education, and therefore they have small need to study especially how to conduct themselves in their intercourse with society. In such cases, their opposition to a written code of manners is rather an affair of theory than of practice, and it seems rather absurd that they should so emphatically denounce the system which they themselves, by example rather than precept, thoroughly carry out. They would be probably as averse to committing any act of rudeness, or any breach of politeness as the warmest admirer of the primitive life of the Indian would be to living himself in a dirty tent, and eating his food, half cooked, on a forked-stick over a camp fire. For such people this little code of the "Laws and By-Laws of American Society" is not written.

There are others who are equally fierce in their denunciations of the ridiculous etiquette above mentioned, but who have not the same natural excuse for being so. These are the rude, rough natures, whom no amount of social rubbing, or intercourse with the most refined would polish, though the professors of the art of good breeding polished never so wisely. They act in their rules of conduct on a principle wholly selfish, making their own ease and comfort the first, if not indeed the sole aim, regardless entirely of the amount of inconvenience or discomfort they may occasion to others. They are obliged to cry down, for mere consistency's sake, the system which condemns their own course of action, and which gives certain laws for governing the conduct, and certain other laws prohibiting many of the acts of rudeness which they find so agreeable, but which others may reasonably object to as offensive. Such persons, too, will of course freely express their opinion, yet their denunciations will probably produce an exactly opposite effect to the one they intend, their own conduct proving the pernicious influence of their theory. Their abuse will be, not the expression, half in badinage, of minds protesting by anticipation against the abuse of forms and ceremonies; but the ignorant invective of coarse-minded people against a principle that would tame them, and mould them into a more agreeable presence. They exclaim loudly against what they personally dislike, however beneficial it may be either to themselves or others. For them this little book of the " Laws and By-Laws of American Society " is not written.

Besides the two classes already mentioned, there is another exceedingly large class of society, which, far from being boorish by nature, yet from circumstances lacks the cultivation which alone will bring the conduct into such training as will fit it practically for exhibition in society. To the persons comprising this class, it is not only a source of regret, but of absolute pain, to be ignorant of the rules which make society cohere, which mark out the functions and duties of the various members which comprise it, and which guard alike against annoyances from the impertinent, and intrusions by the ill-bred, promoting by organized methods the formation of desirable acquaintanceship and pleasant friendships, which otherwise might never take place. Isolation from society, the want of proper instruction, the ill effect of bad example, the advice of the prejudiced, the association with the low-bred, and a hundred other causes, may conspire to prevent that intimacy with the cardinal rules of good behavior, which decorum and good breeding have dictated for the better guidance of the community. It is for such persons, and for the many others who, though not unacquainted with the principles which should guide them in their conduct, are yet often at fault upon questions of detail, and sometimes commit errors, which are the more excusable that absolute rules, deduced from precedent and established by practice alone could set them right, that this code of Modern Etiquette has been prepared. To them it is offered as supplying a need which it is their misfortune, rather than their fault, to experience, in the hope that it will be found to contain a complete guide for them in the open paths and by-paths too of good society.

Before beginning to lay down the rules and ordinances of Etiquette, it will be well to say a few words upon Etiquette itself.

Etiquette is, in point of fact, nothing more nor less than the law, written and unwritten, which regulates the society of civilized people, distinguishing them from the communities of barbarous tribes, whose lives are hard and their manners still harder. It is to a well disciplined and refined mind the fundamental principle of action in all intercourse with society, and they are interested in maintaining it in its integrity, and bound to heed and obey its simplest as well as more formal precepts. The real law-giver is the general convenience, speaking with authority and the experience of many years; and it will be found that even in those cases, where the meaning of its rules may be somewhat obscure at first sight, there is an underlying reason for the regulation laid down.

Etiquette, like every other human institution, is of course liable to abuse; it may be transformed from a convienent and wholesome means of producing universal comfort into an inconvienent and burdensome restraint upon freedom and ease. It may become the first consideration, instead of more properly the second, as is often the case with the instrumental accompaniment to a song, and then it becomes, as does the accompaniment, an intolerable nuisance. The mere form, over-riding and hiding the spirit which should control and guide it; an entirely artificial state of things, taking the place of the natural, must inevitably produce discomfort and extravagance of behavior. Nature is thus made the slave of Art, instead of Art taking its proper place as the handmaid to Nature.

Etiquette, to be perfect, therefore, must be like a perfectly fitting garment, which, beautifying and adorning the person, must yet never cramp or restrain perfect freedom of movement. Any visible restraint will mar its grace, as a wrinkle will mar the pure outline of the garment.

Most people have heard of the gentleman (?) who was perfect in his knowledge of the laws of etiquette, and who, seeing a man drowning, took off his coat and was about to plunge into the water to rescue him, when he suddenly remembered that he had never been introduced to the struggling victim, and resuming his coat, tranquilly proceeded upon his way.

Not less absurd are a thousand instances where a regard for formal mannerism takes the place of the easy grace that is the mark of true politeness, which being well acquired and habitual, is never obtrusive or offensively prominent. Too rigid an observance of the laws of etiquette makes them an absurdity and a nuisance.

But, because the laws of etiquette may be made a restraint under injudicious management, it does not follow that they should be disregarded or in any way set aside. The abuse of them is no argument against them, any more than gluttony is any reason for starvation. It is not the food that is in fault, but the excess of the person partaking of it. The fault must be laid wholly and solely at the door of those who misunderstand the use and intention of really sound and excellent precepts. The extravagance of an over-display of etiquette is really only another form of innate vulgarity, although there are instances which may be drawn from the side of over refinement, from the history of people and societies, who become extravagant in their devotion to what they deem good breeding, simply because, like the stars that looked down upon Molly Bawn, "they'd nothing else to do."

There are to be found, even in grave history—amid the records of war, treaties, conquests, administrations and revolutions—accounts given in equally grave language of deep questions of etiquette which seem to have been debated and settled with as much care and energy as the most serious questions of state affairs. Cases of this sort are announced and well founded. Whoever likes to see the extent to which attention was given to the subject can seek instances in the memoirs of public characters who lived in the seventeenth century, in the diaries of minute detailers like the Duke de St. Simon, Page to His Most Christian Majesty, Louis the Fourteenth; like Sir John Finett, Master of Ceremonies to Charles the First, and in the domestic histories of the courtiers and grandees of the Spanish and Venetian courts.

Fortunately, the time has gone by when nice questions about trifling points of etiquette served to light the flame of civil war, as once they did in France, and to set the whole of the upper class in a kingdom in arms. We owe this, perhaps, as much to the general increase of civilization as to the working of any particular set of rules or system. But the principle which actuated the French nobility, at the time alluded to, is an inherent one in the human mind, and would be likely to repeat itself in some shape or another, not so violently perhaps, but still to repeat itself, were it not kept in check by the known laws of society.

Mr. Buckle tells us that as late as the reign of Louis the Fourteenth, the right to sit in the presence of the French king "was considered to be a matter of such gravity that in comparison with it a mere struggle for liberty faded into insignificance." There was a perpetual striving which should be accounted greatest. According to the old code of etiquette, a duke's wife might sit in the French queen's presence, but no one under that rank could do so. A combination of marquises, counts, and other nobles was formed. and wrung from the hand of Louis the Fourteenth, this concession that the ladies of the house of Bouillon might sit in the presence of the queen. But this was fuel to the fire of the combined noblemen's anger; two hostile parties were formed, and the question of etiquette was nearly being decided by the sword. It required all the tact and statesmanship of Mazarin to prevent this, and in the end the right was conceded to three of the most distinguished ladies of the lower aristocracy, to sit down in the presence of the queen. Upon this, the superior nobility summoned their adherents to Paris, and really a severe struggle followed, which ended in the last mentioned concession being revoked; and so great was the importance attached to the revocation that nothing would satisfy the nobles short of the public withdrawal being drawn up in a state paper, signed by the queen's regent, countersigned by the four secretaries of state, and conveyed to the assembly of nobles by four marshals of France.

The French memoirs of this period (the seventeenth century) abound with references to just such questions of court etiquette; who might use an arm-chair at court; who was to be invited to the royal dinner; who might be kissed by the queen; what degree of nobility entitled a man to be driven to the Louvre in a coach; whether all dukes were equal, or whether, as some thought, the Duke de Bouillon, having once possessed the sovereignty of Sedan, was superior to the Duke de la Rochefoucauld, who had never possessed any sovereignty at all; who should give the king his napkin at dinner, and who might have the honor of assisting at the toilet of the queen. The question whether the Duke de Beaufort ought or ought not to enter the council chamber before the Duke de Nemours, and whether, being there, he ought or ought not to sit above him, caused a violent quarrel between the two dukes in 1652, a quarrel which, of course, ended in a duel, and the death of the Duke de Nemours. The equally grave question, whether a duke should sign before a marshal was violently disputed between the Duke de Rohan and one of the marshals of Henry the Fourth, and the king was obliged to interfere in the matter.

These, of course, are but so many instances of the principle of etiquette carried to an extravagant length, and simply prove the danger there is in allowing things of less importance to supersede or take the precedence of those of greater weight. They serve to explain, and in some measure to excuse the denunciatory expressions which many thoroughly well-bred people use against etiquette, such expressions being, as before suggested, merely protests uttered in anticipation of a repetition of the absurdity which over-attention to ceremonies is liable to introduce.

But such cases are really no argument against etiquette itself, without deference to which it would be impossible to live in anything like freedom from annoyance from persons naturally impertinent, or in the full enjoyment of that social liberty which every one has a right to expect.

Good breeding is, as Lord Chesterfield well says, "the result of much good sense, some good nature, and a little self-denial for the sake of others, and with a view to obtain the same indulgence from them." Lord Bacon, in his admirable essay on Ceremonies, says:

"Not to use ceremonies at all, is to teach others not to use them again, and so diminisheth respect to himself; especially they be not to be omitted to strangers and formal natures; but the dwelling upon them, and exalting them above the moon is not only tedious, but doth diminish the faith and credit of him that speaks."

To quote again from Lord Chesterfield, who says:

"Good sense and good nature suggest civility in general; but in good breeding there are a thousand little delicacies which are established only by custom."

It is precisely these "little delicacies" which constitute the difference between politeness and etiquette. Politeness is that inborn regard for others which may dwell in the heart of the most ignorant boor, but etiquette is a code of outward laws which must be learned by the resident in good society, either from observation or the instruction of others.

It is a poor argument used against etiquette that it is not truthful, and that uncouth manners are more frank and sincere than polished and refined ones. Is truth then a hedgehog, always bristling and offensive. Cannot truth be spoken in courteous accents from a kind, gentle impulse, as well as blurted out rudely and giving pain and mortification? It is true that roughness and sincerity often abide together, but would it destroy the honesty to polish away the roughness?

Etiquette, it is sometimes urged, is used to cloak what is hollow, unmeaning and false, yet may it not also drape gracefully what is true, sincere and important?

True politeness must come from the heart, from an unselfish desire to please others and contribute to their happiness; when upon this natural impulse is placed the polish of a complete and thorough knowledge of the laws of etiquette, the manners must be perfect and graceful.

Etiquette added to natural politeness is as a beautiful jewel upon a tasteful dress. Ruskin thus defines a gentleman:

"A gentleman's first character is that firmness of structure in the body which renders it capable of the most delicate sensation, *and of that structure in the mind which renders it capable of the most delicate sympathies*—one may say simply fineness of nature. This is, of course, compatible with heroic bodily strength and mental firmness; in fact, heroic strength is not conceivable without such delicacy. Elephantine strength may drive its way through a forest, and feel no touch of the boughs, but the white skin of Homer's Atrides would have felt a bent rose leaf, yet subdue its feelings in glow of battle, and behave itself like iron. I do not mean to call an elephant a vulgar animal; but if you think about him carefully, you will find that his non-vulgarity consists in such gentleness as is possible to elephantine nature; not in his insensitive hide, nor in his clumsy foot, but in the way he will lift his foot if a child lies in his way; and in his sensitive trunk, and still more sensitive mind, and capability of pique on points of honor. . . . .

"Hence it will follow, that one of the probable signs of high breeding in men generally will be their kindness and mercifulness; these always indicating more or less firmness of make in the mind."

Undoubtedly the first law of good breeding is unselfishness, that thorough forgetfulness of one's own wants and comforts, and thoughtfulness for the happiness and ease of others, which is the Christian gentleman's rule of life; which makes him yield the easy chair to another older and weaker than himself, and sit upon a narrow bench, or perhaps stand up; which selects for another the choicest portions of the dishes upon the table, and uncomplainingly dines off what is left; which hears with smiling interest the well-worn anecdotes of the veteran story-teller; which gently lifts the little child, who has fallen, and comforts the sobbing grief and terror; which never forgets to endeavor to please others, and seems, at least, pleased with all efforts made to entertain himself. Place the code of politeness beside that of vulgarity and see if the one does not contain all virtue, the other vice. Is not good temper virtuous and polite, bad temper vicious and vulgar? Is not self-denial virtuous and polite, selfishness vicious and vulgar? Is not truth virtuous and polite, scandal vicious and vulgar? Take every principle in the conventional code of the perfectly well-bred, and so define it, and not a virtue is rude.

True etiquette, as we have said before, is not politeness, yet it is founded upon the same basis. An English author says:

"Etiquette may be defined as the minor morality of life. No observances, however minute, that tend to spare the feelings of others, can be classed under the head of trivalities; and politeness, which is but another name for general amiability, will oil the creaking wheels of life more effectually than any of those unguents supplied by mere wealth or station."

To be truly polite, one must be at once good, just and generous, has been well said by a modern French writer.

"True politeness is the outward visible sign of those inward spiritual graces called modesty, unselfishness, generosity. The manners of a gentleman are the index of his soul. His speech is innocent, because his life is pure; his thoughts are direct, because his actions are upright; his bearing is gentle, because his blood, and his impulses, and his training are gentle also. A true gentleman is entirely free from every kind of pretence. He avoids homage, instead of exacting it. Mere ceremonies have no attractions for him. He seeks not only to say civil things, but to do them. His hospitality, though hearty and sincere, will be strictly regulated by his means. His friends will he chosen for their good qualities and good manners; his servants for their thoughtfulness and honesty; his occupations for their usefulness, or their gracefulness, or their elevating tendences, whether moral, or mental, or political. And so we come round again to our first maxims, *i. e.*, that 'good manners are the kindly fruit of a refined nature.'

"And if this be true of mankind, how still more true is it of womankind! Granted that truthfulness, gracefulness, considerateness, unselfishness, are essential to the breeding of a true gentleman, how infinitely essential must they be to the breeding of a true lady! That her tact should be even readier, her sympathies even tenderer, her instinct even finer than those of the man, seems only fit and natural. In her politeness, prevcyance, and all the minor observances of etiquette, are absolutely indispensable. She must be even more upon her guard than a man in all those niceties of speech, look and manner, which are the especial and indispensable credentials of good breeding. Every little drawing-room ceremonial, all the laws of society, the whole etiquette of hospitality must be familiar to her. And even in these points, artificial though they be, her best guide after all, is that kindness of heart which gives honor where honor is due, and which is ever anxious to spare the feelings and prejudices of others.

"Every mistress of a house, be it remembered, is a minor sovereign, upon whose bounty the comfort, and happiness, and refinement of her little court depends. She must take especial care that her servants are capable, well trained and reliable, and that her domestic arrangements are carried on as noiselessly and easily as if by machinery. In a well ordered house the machinery is always in order, and always works out of sight. No well-bred woman talks of her servants, of her dinner arrangements, or the affairs of her nursery. One feels these matters to be under her *surveillance*, and that fact alone is a guarantee of their good management. The amusements and comforts of her guests are provided for without discussion or comment; and whatever goes wrong is studiously withheld from the conversation of the drawing-room. And let no lady, however young, however beautiful, however gifted, for one moment imagine that the management of her house can be neglected with impunity. If she is rich enough to provide an efficient housekeeper, well and good; but, even so, the final responsibility must still rest upon her, and her alone. No tastes, no pleasures must stand in the way of this important duty; and even if that duty should at first seem irksome, the fulfillment of it is sure to bring its own reward.

"The very atmosphere of the house proclaims the mistress. The servants wear a cheerful air, and meet you with candid and friendly faces; the rooms are tastefully furnished; an irreproachable cleanliness and neatness reign around. The unexpected guest finds an orderly table and an unembarrassed welcome. In such a house, scandal finds no favor, and conversation never degenerates into gossip. In such a home, peace and plenty and goodwill are permanent household gods."

The most perfect law of politeness, the safest and surest guide in all that pertains to the true definition of a gentleman or lady is, after all, the Christian rule—

"Do unto others as you would others should do unto you."

No one with this for a guide can ever fail in true, genuine *politeness*, and that politeness will soon lead him to learn and remember all the prevailing rules of established *etiquette*.

INTRODUCTIONS.

NEVER introduce people to each other unless you are sure the acquaintance so commenced will be mutually agreeable.

A person who, from youth, social position or any other cause, stands in the inferior position of the two persons to be introduced to each other, must be introduced to the superior. A gentleman is always to be introduced to a lady, never a lady to a gentleman.

At a ball, it is the part of the host and hostess to make introductions amongst the guests; but guests may with perfect propriety introduce friends to each other. Gentlemen must never introduce friends to ladies, without first obtaining special permission to do so, and this permission should be always granted, unless there is a very strong reason for the refusal. The French, and in a great measure the English, dispense with introductions at a private ball. It is taken for granted that the hostess has invited to her ball only such people as are fit to be mutually acquainted, and the fact that they have been invited to meet each other is a sufficient warrant for self-introduction. This practice saves a great deal of trouble, but it applies only to balls in private houses. At any public ball, partners must be introduced to each other; indeed it is better for ladies at such entertainments, to dance only with the gentlemen of their own party, or with whom they had a previous acquaintance. Special introductions may, however, be made with propriety by the master of ceremonies.

When introducing two gentlemen, look first to the elder, or, if there is any difference in social standing, to the superior, and with a slight bow say to him: "Allow me to introduce my friend, Mr. Jones, to you;" then turning to your friend, repeat his name, and follow it by that of the gentleman to whom he is introduced, thus: "Mr. Smith, allow me to introduce my friend, Mr. Jones, to you—Mr. Jones, Mr. Smith." In introducing a gentleman to a lady, bow slightly to the latter, saying, "Miss ——, allow me to introduce Mr. ——; Mr. ——, (bowing to him) Miss ——."

When several persons are introduced to one, it is sufficient to name the single individual once, repeating all the names of the others, thus: "Mr. Johnson, allow me to introduce Mr. and Mrs. James, Miss Smithson, Mr. Lewis, Mr. Johnson," bowing slightly to each when named.

Shaking hands after an introduction has taken place is merely optional, not necessary; and is forbidden to an unmarried lady to whom a gentleman is introduced. A bow is all that etiquette requires. In introducing young persons to elder ones of good social standing, it is often a kindly act of encouragement for the latter to shake hands, with a few cordial words.

It is not necessary to introduce people who meet at your house on morning calls, though it may be done with propriety if the introduction has been previously ascertained to be mutually pleasant.

It is optional after such an introduction, with the parties introduced, to continue or drop the acquaintance so formed. Without a formal introduction, the merely meeting at the house of a mutual friend, does not warrant any future recognition. It rests, however, after an introduction with the lady, if between lady and gentleman, with the married or elder lady, if between lady and lady, and with the elder, if between gentlemen, to continue or drop the acquaintance.

Gentlemen who meet at the house or rooms of a mutual friend are not obliged to recognize one another if they meet again elsewhere. There is no rule forbidding their doing so, if agreeable to both parties, but there is no requirement of etiquette obliging them to appear as if they had even met before.

A lady is not obliged to afterwards recognize a partner with whom she may have danced at a ball. It is entirely optional with her to do so or not; and if she has danced several times with the gentlemen, it will be a question between her and her conscience how far she may consider herself justified in passing by without notice one who has extended to her so much courtesy at a ball. Etiquette, however, does not require even the slightest recognition.

When strangers in a city are introduced to residents it is customary to name the place from which they come, thus: "Allow me to introduce to you my friend Mr. Schmidt, from Germany—Mr. Schmidt, Mr. Popking;" or if introducing a traveller, "Allow me to introduce my friend Mr. Robinson, lately returned from Egypt." A pleasant opening is thus offered for conversation, and a foreigner may have the pleasure of a salutation in his own language.

An important duty in introducing friends is to pronounce the name of each party clearly and distinctly, that no error or necessity for repetition may occur.

It is often a positive kindness to take advantage of the etiquette which dispenses with introductions at morning calls. Many a witty, talented person has had a stupid bore pursue him upon such an introduction, and even the one necessary conversation following an introduction is a painful effort, owing to the entire uncongeniality of the parties introduced.

A friend visiting at your house must be introduced to all callers, who are bound to continue the acquaintance as long as the friend is your guest. So, if when calling upon a friend, you are introduced to a visitor, you are bound to extend all courtesies and attentions which you would desire paid to your visitors in similar circumstances.

Introductions, given at a party to a stranger visiting in a city, must be followed by recognition as long as the visit continues.

If, when walking with one friend, you should meet another, it is not necessary to introduce them; indeed, you should not do so without special reason for it. Never, even after an introduction, start a long conversation, unless all continue the walk in the same direction.

Should you, when walking with a friend, meet a lady who desires to speak to you, your friend must stop with you, yet an introduction under such circumstances does not exact any future recognition.

Sisters, brothers or other relatives may always be introduced to friends when met casually.

If friends meet at public places of amusement and are accompanied by strangers, introductions are not required by etiquette, and if made do not oblige any future acquaintance.

It is not necessary to have an introduction in order to pay your respects to the President of the United States, excepting that of the master of ceremonies at the receptions. He will receive your card and present you. For a private interview it is better to be introduced by a Senator or a member of the House of Representatives.

In visiting foreign courts, introductions are more a matter of ceremony than in this country. If you wish to obtain an introduction to the Emperor of France, you must address your request to the Grand Chamberlain, which may be done personally or by letter.

Your statement that you are an American citizen, and a reference to the American Consul will procure you an interview. Punctuality to the hour appointed for the interview is essential, and ladies present themselves in full dress; gentlemen in a dress suit of black, white vest, gloves and neck-tie.

The ceremony of presentation will be explained before you are presented.

In the English court, the ladies must be presented by a lady; gentlemen by a gentleman. Strangers must have credentials from the Consul before they can be introduced.

If at a dinner, a ball, or upon any occasion you are introduced, at a friend's house, to one with whom you are not on good terms, though it be your bitterest enemy, etiquette requires you to salute him or her courteously, and make no sign of resentment whilst under your friend's roof.

If you are introduced as a petitioner to any one in authority, that introduction does not authorize you in claiming an acquaintance afterwards.

Never introduce persons who may be related to you, without calling their full name. It is done very often, even amongst well-bred people, from thoughtfulness, as, "Mrs. James, allow me to introduce my cousin Frank; Frank, Mrs. James," and poor Mrs. James is left entirely ignorant of cousin Frank's name. The proper way is to name the relationship and also the surname of the relative. If you introduce a brother or sister even, marriage may have changed the name of one. You should say: "Mrs. James, allow me to introduce to you my sister, Miss Curtis; Miss Curtis, Mrs. James."

If you are introduced to the relative of a friend, etiquette requires you to consider that relative an acquaintance, unless there is some special reason to the contrary.

It is best to avoid introductions in a public conveyance, as few people like to have their names called out in such places. If such introductions are made, however, it should be done as quietly as possible.

To introduce to a friend a person who is in any way objectionable, is an insult which fully justifies a withdrawal of friendship.

A gentleman should always raise his hat, if introduced in the street, to either lady or gentleman.

If introducing a foreigner or a gentleman in this country, whose position gives him an honorary title, always give the title. Thus, if a member of Congress, meeting a German baron at your house, you introduce them, you say: "Mr. Somers, allow me to introduce to you my friend, the Baron von Schmidt; Baron von Schmidt, the Honorable Mr. Somers."

LETTERS OF INTRODUCTION.

LETTERS of introduction should never be given, except to persons well known to the person introducing them, and addressed to those only who have a long-standing friendship for the writer. Amongst persons but slightly acquainted, such letters are not only foolish but positively dangerous, as you may thus give your countenance to those who will take advantage of your carelessness to bring you into mortifying, if not disgraceful positions.

Even amongst friends of long standing they should be given very cautiously and sparingly, as it is a great responsibility to send to your friend a visitor who may prove disagreeable, and you have no right whatever to call upon comparative strangers to extend hospitality or courtesy to your friends.

Letters of introduction should always be as short and concise as possible. If you wish to send any information to your friends about their visitor, send it in a separate letter by mail.

The utmost brevity is of importance in the letter of introduction, as it is usually read in the presence of the party introduced, and the pause must necessarily be awkward. You may in a letter of introduction use a few words of warm, cordial feeling toward your friend, but praise of any kind is in as bad taste as it would be at a personal introduction.

This rule, however, does not apply to letters introducing applicants for favor, office or position, which latter come more strictly under the head of letters of recommendation than merely letters of introduction.

Letters of introduction must be left unsealed invariably; they should be folded and addressed like any other letter, but it is a gross breach of etiquette to prevent the bearer from reading what you may have said of him to your friend. It is optional with the bearer to seal such letters before delivery, but it is customary to leave them open.

A letter of introduction should not, unless circumstances make it absolutely unavoidable, be delivered in person. It should be sent, with the card of the person introduced, to the person to whom it is addressed, by a servant. The person receiving it should then call at once or send a written invitation to his house, and the person introduced may then call in person. If, however, the stay in the city is very short, these formalities must be omitted, and the person introduced call in person, sending in his letter and card by a servant.

Business letters of introduction should mention the errand and business of the party introduced, and if your own acquaintance is of recent date, mention by whom your were yourself introduced.

Letters introducing professional artists may contain a few words expressive of the pleasure conferred by the talent or skill of the person introduced.

Letters of introduction soliciting favors should be but seldom given, and never unless the claims upon both parties interested are very strong.

There is no rule of etiquette prescribing the exact amount of attention required to be shown to the bearer of a letter of introduction by the person to whom it is addressed.

A thousand circumstances of time, place, position, leisure and disposition of the parties must control this, but as a rule, the most generous hospitality and courtesy it is possible to give, should be extended to your friend's friend. It is a compliment to both the bearer and the writer of the letter. La Fontaine says: "A letter of introduction is a draft at sight, and you must cash it." It might be added, "You must cash it in full, never allowing the courtesy exchange to be against the presenter of the draft."

Letters of introduction should bear upon the envelope the name and address of the party introduced, written in the left hand corner—thus:

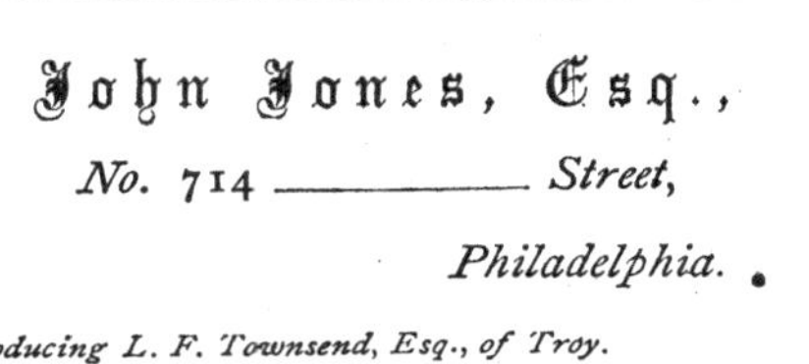
John Jones, Esq.,
No. 714 ———— Street,
Philadelphia.
Introducing L. F. Townsend, Esq., of Troy.

Letters of introduction to and from business men, for business purposes, may be delivered by the bearers in person, and etiquette does not require the receiver to entertain the person introduced as the private friend of the writer. Good nature and native courtesy would suggest some attentions, which could be increased according to the pleasure conferred or received, but it is entirely optional.

Letters of introduction are very useful to travellers, or those about to change their place of residence; care, however, should be especially taken in the latter case to present persons to each other only, who will prove mutually agreeable, as it is surely no friendly act to force upon your friends a life-long acquaintance, perhaps with uncongenial persons.

A form is given for an ordinary letter of introduction, to be varied according to circumstances, always bearing in mind that brevity is essential, long acquaintance necessary, and some claim on both parties important, before giving any letters of introduction to your friends and acquaintances.

"New York, August 12, 1869.

"James Wilcox, Esq.,

"*Dear Sir*:—Allow me to introduce to you my friend, Mr. Loving, who will make a brief visit to your city. Any attention you may be able to show him, during his stay, will be appreciated as a favor by,

"Yours sincerely,

"E. B. Lyons."

(To be directed) "James Wilcox, Esq.,
"No. 204 —— Street,
"Washington, D. C.
"Introducing F. G. Loving, Esq., of New York."

In receiving such a letter, bear in mind the courtesy extended is really a compliment to the writer of the letter, and such hospitality and courtesy as you extend you are entitled to claim again for your own friends at some future time. If you are in a position to do so, you should follow your first call by an invitation to dinner, or to meet friends in the evening, and if the new comer is a stranger in the city, select such friends to meet him or her, as will prove agreeable and valuable acquaintances. If your are a bachelor or boarding, and cannot extend the hospitalities of a home, offer your services as guide to points of interest in the city, places of public amusement, in short, extend any courtesy your purse or leisure time will warrant.

It is contrary to etiquette for the bearer of a letter of introduction to visit too frequently the house to which he has just been introduced. The fact that Mr. Smith is your only friend in town, and has been cordial in his invitations to "make his house your home," does not justify you in pulling too frequently at Mr. Smith's door-bell, or presenting yourself at unseasonable hours in Mrs. Smith's drawing-room.

In travelling abroad it is impossible to have too many letters of introduction. They take up but little room in a trunk, but their value when you find yourself "a stranger in a strange land," cannot be over-estimated.

SALUTES AND SALUTATIONS.

In this country men do not embrace each other, nor do they exchange kisses, while, unless amongst intimate friends, even the fair sex now dispense with demonstrative salutations. In many European countries kisses are exchanged, even between gentlemen, and an embrace is quite in accordance with even a somewhat formal salutation. In America, however, these demonstrations are mostly confined to gushing misses and school-girls.

Men in this country acknowledge an introduction by extending the right hand in greeting—the whole hand—for it is positively insulting to offer two fingers, as some under-bred snobs will sometimes do, and it is almost as bad to extend the left hand, unless two persons are introduced at the same time, or the right hand is useless or occupied; in any such case apologize for the hand extended. The right hand is the sword hand, and its extension to a friend is emblematic as a proof of peace, and as a safeguard against treachery.

In offering the hand to a friend in the house, always remove the glove, and grasp the hand given in return firmly for a moment. In the street, however, the glove may be retained, if it would cause an awkward pause to remove it; but always in such a case apologize for the covered hand.

In shaking hands, do not try to wring them off the wrists, nor press them as in a vise, nor pull them as though they were bell-handles, nor fling the two together with violence, so as to cause a report. Let the palms grasp each other firmly, but without any display of energy, and shake the hand moderately for a moment, then release it. Mr. Pecksniff was wont to clasp his left hand over his " dear friend's " right hand, resting in his own right. This practice may be very effective, from a scenic point of view, but it is not countenanced by any rule of etiquette.

A lady must first recognize a gentleman by bowing before he is at liberty to salute her. She is the sole judge of the propriety of recognizing him at all, and etiquette requires the strictest deference to her desire in this respect. Should she recognize him, he should raise his hat a little from his head, with the hand furthest from her, and return her salutation with a slight inclination of the body. He may not obtrude himself upon her notice even if he thinks she has not observed him.

A lady should never stop in the street to salute a gentleman friend, nor may a gentleman join a lady in the street.

Should a lady, however, stop in meeting a gentleman, etiquette requires him to stop also, no matter how great his haste. If he is really unable to stop any time, he must at least pause long enough to state this fact, and apologize for leaving her in such haste.

When a lady wishes to end a conversation in the street, she should bow slightly, and the gentleman must at once take his leave.

If a lady resumes her walk without any pause in the conversation, a gentleman is then at liberty to join her in her promenade.

Married ladies are allowed more freedom in such matters than unmarried ones. It is against all established laws of etiquette for young unmarried ladies to do more than bow to gentlemen in the street, unless the fact of relationship allows some violation of strict etiquette.

Unless related, or upon terms of intimate friendship with a gentleman, a lady should never salute excepting by a slightly formal bow. A nod is vulgar, even when exchanged by intimate friends.

In her own house, however, a lady should extend her hand in salutation to every guest who crosses her threshold.

Froissart, that charmingly quaint writer, tells of the dame of ancient days thus :

" When Sir Walter Manny and his men returned from a successful sortie out of Henneboune, the chronicle tells us, ' The Countess de Montfort came down from the castle to meet them, and with a most cheerful countenance kissed Sir Walter Manny and all his companions, one after the other, like a noble and valiant dame.' " Modern etiquette would hardly speak in praise of such a lady in the current year.

On horseback a lady salutes by bowing slightly. A gentleman, grasping reins and whip in his left hand, raises his hat slightly with his right, at the same time inclining the body forward. He

may not, however, join a lady riding, unless she is escorted only by a groom, and then he must first request permission to do so.

Never will a gentleman so far imitate a vulgar clown as to smack a friend on the back, poke him in the ribs, or by clapping his hand upon his shoulder. It is equally bad taste to use a familiar shout, or "Hullo, old boy!" or any other "Hail fellow, well met" phrase of salutation.

If a gentleman salutes another by mistake, even if he has given him an unceremonious slap or poke, it is etiquette to treat the offender with the utmost courtesy. He will probably be sufficiently embarrassed, when he discovers his error, without having any blunt speech made to add to his discomfiture.

If a gentleman meet a gentleman, he may salute him by touching his hat without removing it, but if a lady be with either gentleman both hats must be lifted in salutation.

If a gentleman stops to speak to a lady, in the street, he must hold his hat in his hand during the interview, unless she requests him to replace it. With a gentleman friend etiquette does not require this formality.

A gentleman may bow to a lady seated at a window, if he is passing on the street, but he must not bow from a window to a lady on the street.

A gentleman may never offer to shake hands with a lady, but he must accept such an offer on her part, taking her hand lightly but firmly in his ungloved right one, and delicately shaking it for a moment. A pressure is an insult in such a case.

In entering a church a gentleman must remove his hat as soon as his foot crosses the threshold of the sacred edifice. Travellers will often omit this salutation in visiting churches abroad, whose faith differs from their own. There is no more certain sign of ill-breeding as well as irreverence.

A gentleman may always bow to a lady he may meet on a stairway, even if not acquainted. If at the foot of the stairs, he must bow, pass her and ascend before her. If at the head of the stairs, he must bow, and wait for her to precede him in the descent.

If two friends are walking together and meet a friend of one, a bow is all the salutation etiquette demands; if, however, one of the two stops to speak to the third, he owes the friend he accompanies an apology for the delay thus occasioned.

In entering a room, a gentleman must take his hat, cane and gloves in his left hand, leaving his right hand free for salutation.

If a gentleman, walking with a friend, meets a lady with whom his friend is acquainted, he must also bow, although the lady may be a stranger to him. The bow must be very slight and formal, merely, in fact, a compliment to his friend, and a mark of respect to the lady.

A gentleman must always return a bow made to him in the street, even if he fails to recognize the person who makes it. It may be a person to whom he has been introduced, but whose face he has forgotten, and if it is an error on the part of the other, a courteous return of the salute will greatly diminish the embarrassment of the mistaken party.

In meeting a party of friends with some of whom you are intimately acquainted, and with some only slightly, endeavor to make your salutations as equal as possible. A formal bow to one, and a gushing demonstration of delight over another is a breach of etiquette. Be courteous and cordial to all.

If a foreigner salute you after the fashion of his own country, do not draw back or allow yourself to smile, but strive to put him at his ease by taking no notice of the "national salute."

Kissing in public, even between intimate lady friends, is a vulgar parade of affection, that a truly refined person will shrink from.

It is an insult to return a cordial grasp of the hand, and hearty greeting, by a cold bow or a flabby extension of a portion of the hand. Even if you do not approve of the familiar geeting you should return it with some show of cordiality.

The Countess de ——, speaking of salutations, says:

"It would seem that good manners were originally the mere expression of submission from the weaker to the stronger. In a rude state of society every salutation is to this day an act of worship. Hence the commonest acts, phrases and signs of courtesy with which we are now familiar, date from those earlier stages when the strong hand ruled, and the inferior demonstrated his allegiance by studied servility. Let us take for example the words 'Sir' and 'Madam.' 'Sir' is derived from Seigneur, Sieur, Sire, and originally meant Lord, King, Ruler, and in its patriarchal sense, Father. The title of Sire was last borne by some of the ancient feudal families of France who, as Selden has said, 'affected rather to be styled by the name of Sire than Baron, as Le Sire de Montmorenci and the like.'

"Madam or Madame, corrupted by servants into 'Ma'am,' and by Mrs. Gamp and her tribe into 'Mum,' is in substance equivalent to 'Your exalted,' or 'Your Highness.' *Ma Dame* originally meaning high-born or stately, and being applied only to ladies of the highest rank.

"To turn to our every-day forms of salutation. We take off our hats on visiting an acquaintance. We bow on being introduced to strangers. We rise when visitors enter our drawing-room. We wave our hand to our friends as he passes the window, or drives away from our door. The Oriental, in like manner, leaves his shoes on the threshold when he pays a visit. The natives of the Tonga Islands kiss the soles of a chieftain's feet. The Siberian peasant grovels in the dust before a Russian noble. Each of these acts has a primary, a historical significance. The very word 'salution' in the first place, derived as it is from 'salutatio,' the daily homage paid by a Roman client to his patron, suggests in itself a history of manners.

"To bare the head was originally an act of submission to gods and rulers. A bow is a modified protestation. A lady's courtesy is a modified genuflexion. Rising and standing are acts of homage; and when we wave our hand to the friend on the opposite side of the street, we are unconsciously imitating the Romans who, as Selden tells us, used to stand 'somewhat off before the images of their gods, solemnly moving the right hand to the lips and casting it, as if they had cast kisses.'

"Again, men remove the glove when they shake hands with a lady—a custom evidently of feudal origin. The knight removed his iron gauntlet, the pressure of which would have been all too harsh for the palm of a fair *chatelaine*, and the custom which began in necessity has travelled down to us as a point of etiquette."

General salutations of a mixed company are not now in vogue in the best society, where etiquette requires that we recognize only our own friends and acquaintances.

In meeting at a friend's house where you are visiting a circle who are all entire strangers to you, remember that as mutual friends of the host and hostess you are bound whilst under the same roof to consider yourselves as acquaintances. No spirit of exclusiveness is an apology for a neglect of this, and no shyness can excuse a withdrawing into a corner, or clinging to one friend alone in such a circle.

CALLS.

When ladies have, according to the French custom, set apart one morning or one evening in the week for receiving callers, it is a breach of etiquette to call at any other time, unless a short visit in the city or business that will not admit of delay are the excuses. An hour in the evening, and from ten to twenty minutes in the morning are the limits for a formal call.

When there is no time thus set apart, formal calls must be paid in the morning, but with friends of long standing the evening call is not only permissible, but often far more welcome.

Morning calls may be made by gentlemen in society upon all the occasions following:

In answer to a letter of introduction sent to him, or to return the call if the letter is personally presented.

In return for any hospitality offered to him when visiting another city, if the entertainer visit his own place of abode.

In return for any favor received or courtesy extended to him by another gentleman.

In return for an invitation to the house of a friend, whether the invitation has been accepted or declined, and this call must be made within the week following that during which the entertainment was given.

On any occasion when a grief or a joy calls for expressions of condolence or congratulation in the circle of his friends.

To greet the safe return of any friend who has been abroad, or away from home for any length of time.

Following any occasion when a lady has accepted his services as an escort, a gentleman must call to inquire after the health of his fair charge, and must not delay longer than the day after that upon which he has escorted the lady.

After a wedding, at the time appointed for the reception of friends.

When visiting in another city, upon any friends there, or upon those to whom letters of introduction have been given.

In asking or granting a favor, a call is demanded by etiquette.

The visit or call is a much better institution than the vulgar suppose. It is not without its objections, consuming valuable time, and giving occasion for gossip and small talk, but it is the most agreeable and customary way of turning a mere acquaintance into a friend. In a friendly call much of the restraint of meeting in large assemblies is thrown aside, mind meets mind much more easily in an easy *tête a tête* conversation, and the conversation may be allowed to partake somewhat more of a personal character than it could in the ball-room or evening party.

First calls require prompt return, even if you drop the acquaintance before the second one.

Morning calls must never be earlier than noon, evening ones never later than nine o'clock.

When calling, if the room seems crowded, do not prolong your visit.

A gentleman may never call with a friend upon a lady, unless the friend is previously acquainted, or he has obtained permission of the lady to introduce him.

In making a formal call, a gentleman must retain his hat in his hand. An umbrella or cane may be left in the hall, never the hat or gloves. If the call is made in the evening, the hat and gloves must be held until the host or hostess gives an invitation to lay them aside and spend the evening. Strict etiquette requires that such an invitation shall not be given, or if given, not accepted on the occasion of a first call.

In making an informal call in the evening, a gentleman may leave hat, gloves, cane and overcoat in the hall.

No gentleman will prolong a call if he finds his host or hostess dressed to go out. A brief visit with a promise to repeat it will place his entertainers at ease, and even if they urge a longer stay, the very fact that they were preparing to go out, proves their desire to do so.

A card used in calling must never have anything upon it, but the name and address of the caller. Nothing can show a greater ignorance of the customs of society than to use a business card for a friendly call. A physician may put the prefix Dr. or the professional M.D., upon his card, and an Army or Navy officer his rank and branch of service. Thus a civilian's card must be simply:

JAMES LAWTON,
417 L—— Street.

A physician's:

DR. JEROME HAYES,
218 T—— Street, or

JEROME HAYES, M.D.

An Army officer's:

LIEUT. JAMES BENNETT,
U. S. A.

An Naval officer's:

LIEUT. HENRY KEYSER,
U. S. N.

In receiving a gentleman caller, a gentleman meets him at the door, takes his hat and cane, and places a chair for him, but a lady does not leave her seat to receive a gentleman, slightly rising to bow, and resuming her place again when her visitor is seated; in receiving another lady, a lady should rise and advance to meet her, also rise and accompany her to the door when leaving, unless she has other callers, in which case, she is not required to leave her place, only standing to bid her caller farewell.

And English authority gives some excellent directions for calling upon occasions of congratulation or condolence. He says:

"Visits of condolence and congratulation must be made about a week after the event. If you are intimate with the person upon whom you call, you may ask, in the first case, for admission; if not, it is better to leave only a card, and make your "kind inquiries" of the servant, who is generally primed in what manner to answer them. In visits of congratulation you should always go in, and be hearty in your congratulations. Visits of condolence are terrible inflictions to both receiver and giver, but they may be made less so by avoiding, as much as is consistent with sympathy, any allusion to the past. The receiver does well to abstain from tears. A lady of my acquaintance, who had lost her husband, was receiving such a visit in her best crape. She wept profusely for sometime upon the best broad hemmed cambric handkerchiefs, and then turning to her visitor said: 'I am sure that you will be glad to hear that Mr. B. has left me most comfortably provided for.' *Hinc illæ lachrymæ.* Perhaps they would have been more sincere if he had left her without a penny. At the same time, if you have not sympathy and heart enough to pump up a little condolence, you will do better to avoid it, but take care that your conversation is not too gay. Whatever you may feel you must respect the sorrows of others.

"On marriage, cards are sent round to such people as you wish to keep among your acquaintances, and it is then their part to call first on the young couple, when within distance."

A lady when calling keeps her parasol in her hand, and is not required to remove her glove.

No dog, however "dear or interesting," can be admitted to the drawing-room, and it is bad taste to have one follow you from home, if you intend to make calls.

It is better for a lady not to have a child with her when paying calls, unless it is trained to sit silent, or old enough to behave with quiet propriety.

It is a sign of low-breeding to fidget with the hat, cane or parasol during a call. They are introduced merely as signs that the caller is in walking dress, and are not intended, the hat to be whirled round the top of the cane, the cane to be employed in tracing out the pattern of the carpet, or the parasol to be tapped on the teeth, or worse still, sucked.

It is in bad taste for a caller to preface his or her departure by consulting a watch, remarking, "Now I must go," or insinuating that the hostess is weary of the visitor. Rise when ready to go, and express your pleasure at finding your friends at home, followed by a cordially expressed desire for a speedy meeting again.

Pelham said he always withdrew when he said something that produced a sensation, because he knew he must leave such an impression as would make people wish to see him again.

The lady of the house should always ring when visitors rise to go, that a servant may be ready to show them out.

When other callers arrive, it is in bad taste to rise at once as if

driven away. Let the first caller watch for a favorable opportunity to retire gracefully.

If a gentleman calling sees a lady unescorted rise to go, he may with perfect propriety offer to escort her to her carriage, even if a stranger, but he must return again to make his own farewell bow to the hostess.

The most trivial subjects are admissible for a call, and it is not in good taste to discuss deep interests, political questions or matters of grave moment.

If strangers are in the room when a caller rises to leave, courtesy requires only a slight bow in passing.

When calling, etiquette requires that a card be sent up. It will show that you have called, and if friends are at home, will prevent any confusion from mispronunciation of your name by the servant.

When the lady of the house is not at home, a card must be left, and if there are two or more ladies, the turning down of one corner of the card signifies that the call was intended for all the family.

If cards to be left preparatory to leaving town, the initials p. p. c. (*pour prendre congé*,* or, presents parting compliments), must be written in the left hand corner. If the departure is a hurried one, the card may be sent by a servant, but it is in better taste to leave in it person.

Cards sent during the illness of any member of the family to whom they are sent, must be accompanied by verbal inquiries regarding the patient's health. The same rule applies to the survivors when cards of condolence are sent.

Cards may be left or sent the day after a ball or large evening party.

After a dinner party or small social gathering, cards must be left within the following week. When unable to accept an invitation to dinner, a call should soon afterwards be made to express regret at the inability to be present.

Visits of condolence are made within a week after the bereavement, unless the deceased be one of the immediate family, when a fortnight may be allowed to intervene. Cards may, however, be left immediately after the death is known.

The first call of a stranger must be returned within a week.

* To take leave.

Married men are not obliged to make calls of ceremony in person. It is sufficient for their wives to leave their cards with their own.

Residents in a place make the first call upon any new comers.

If a lady does not wish to receive visitors, her servant must be instructed to reply "not at home," to callers. This is not meant to imply that she is out of the house; merely that she is not home to callers. To say that she is "engaged" answers the same purpose, but such answers must be made upon the first inquiry, for if the visitor is announced, he or she may conclude the refusal is intended for that especial call.

It is not necessary, nor is it customary in the city, to offer refreshments to callers. In the country, especially if the visitors have come from a distance, it is not only courteous, but often a positive kindness to do so.

If a stranger come to stay at the house of a friend, those who are in the habit of visiting at the house should call as soon as possible, and such calls should be returned at the earliest practicable opportunity.

A well-bred person should endeavor to be always prepared for callers. If it is impossible, during the day, to see your friends, instruct your servant to deny them at the door, but if once within house, no personal inconvenience should prevent you from presenting yourself. Illness alone, either your own, or that of some one requiring your constant attention, can then excuse you.

A lady should avoid keeping callers waiting. If they call before the hours etiquette has appointed, it is better to see them in the morning dress than to make them wait for a more elaborate toilet. If there is any fault, it is their own for intruding at improper hours.

Persons who do not keep a carriage should not make visits of ceremony in wet weather. It is ill-bred to enter a drawing-room, with a handsome carpet upon it, in muddy boots and spattered garments, to stand a dripping umbrella beside you, or deposit over-shoes in the hall.

Never resume your seat after having once left it to say adieu. There is nothing more awkward than to take leave twice.

A lady who is receiving morning visits, may keep some trifling fancy-work in her hand, if she desires; but drawing, music, writing or any other absorbing occupation must at once be laid aside.

In receiving many callers at one time, a well-bred lady must divide her attentions as equally as possible. A *tête a tête* conversation is a gross breach of etiquette, and no one may receive any especial notice excepting any elderly person.

If, during a call any *contretemps* occur, shorten your visit. Your hostess may preserve a smiling serenity while a voice in the distance proclaims that, "Johnnie has fallen down the stairs," or "Mary has set the nursery curtains on fire," but you may be certain she will not resent your departure, even if you have not been two minutes seated.

If you find yourself intruding upon an early dinner hour, do not prolong your stay.

A call may be made upon a friend to whom some good fortune has come, as promotion in service or other happy event, even if he has not returned the last of your visits.

It is a breach of etiquette, during a call, to draw near to the fire to warm your hands and feet, unless you are invited by the mistress of the house to do so. If you are alone in the drawing-room for a time, while your visit is announced, and then go to the fire, leave your seat and advance to meet the mistress of the house as she enters, and then take the seat she points out to you.

In visiting an invalid, never offer to go to the room, but wait for an invitation to do so.

A gentleman who is a confirmed invalid, may receive the visits of a lady friend, but under no other circumstances.

Calls made either in person or by card, during an illness of your own, must be returned as soon as you are able to go abroad again.

It is a breach of etiquette to remove the gloves when making a formal call.

It is a breach of etiquette to stare round a room when you are making a call.

In paying visits of condolence, let your dress be subdued. It is offensive to put on your gayest attire to call upon a friend in affliction, and equally so to converse upon such subjects as balls, opera or similar amusements. Let the mourner decide whether to speak of the recent sorrow or not.

A lady who allows remarks to be made upon a caller, who has just left the room, commits not only a breach of etiquette, but a positive rudeness and ill-natured act. It is quite easy to check any such disposition by a grave reserve, and to turn the conversation at once.

Calls in the country may be less ceremonious, and of longer duration than those in the city.

It is an ostentation almost unkind for a lady to call upon a friend in reduced circumstances, with any parade of her own wealth in equipage or dress.

No mistress of the house may ever leave the room when there are visitors in it.

It is a breach of etiquette for a caller, who is waiting the entrance of the hostess, to open the piano, or to touch it if it is open.

It is a breach of etiquette to walk round the room when waiting for your hostess, examining the furniture or pictures.

It is a breach of etiquette for a caller to open or shut a door, raise or lower a window curtain, or in any way alter the arrangement of a room.

Many consider a clock on a drawing-room mantel a breach of etiquette, as it seems to hint to visitors to keep early hours.

It is a breach of etiquette to turn your chair so as to bring your back to any one seated near to you.

It is a breach of etiquette when making a call, to play with any ornament in the room, finger the furniture, or seem indeed to be aware of anything but the company present.

To prolong a call to the next meal time is a positive rudeness, as it forces your hostess to invite you to the table whether convenient and agreeable or not.

In calling upon friends at a boarding-house or a hotel, always write their names above your own upon your card, that it may be certain to be delivered to the right person.

CONVERSATION.

There are several principal rules of etiquette which must be rigidly observed in conversation, the non-observance of which will at once stamp the guilty party as ignorant of the forms and customs of polite society.

Ungrammatical expressions are unfortunately too common even amongst those who have not the excuse of ignorance, but who fall into the use of them merely from carelessness, or unconscious imitation of others. "Says she to me," and other vulgarisms of a like type, are also a gross violation of good taste in conversation.

The personal pronouns should be used as little as possible when speaking of any one, either present or absent. The name of the lady or gentleman to whom reference is made should be repeated if necessary, but under no circumstances should the words "she" or "he," accompanied by a nod or jerk of the thumb, in the direction of the person spoken of, be employed. Never talk of any one with whom you may have held intercourse as "that party," or "a party" of your acquaintance.

Avoid as utterly hateful the use of slang terms. There are surely words enough in the English language to express all the thoughts and ideas of the mind, and it is a sign of pure vulgarity to employ synonyms, the only remarkable part of which is that they derive their existence solely from vulgar sources. In a gentleman such expressions are too suggestive of low company, and intercourse with the worst associates, and in a lady such expressions are too offensive to be tolerated at all in good society. Slang never ornamented conversation, but it invariably sullies and degrades it. Equally to be censured as a violation of etiquette, and more so in a moral point of view, is the use of profanity; it is a sure mark, not only of low-breeding, but of a narrow, degraded if not a positively vicious mind. Lamont says:

"Whatever fortune may be made by perjury, I believe there never was a man who made a fortune by common swearing. It often appears that men pay for swearing, but it seldom happens that they are paid for it. It is not easy to perceive what honor or credit is connected with it. Does any man receive promotion because he is a notable blusterer? Or is any man advanced to dignity because he is expert at profane swearing? Never. Low must be the character which such impertinence will exalt: high must be the character which such impertinence will not degrade. Inexcusable, therefore, must be the practice which has neither reason nor passion to support it. The drunkard has his cups; the satirist his revenge; the ambitious man his preferments; the miser his gold; but the common swearer has nothing; he is a fool at large, sells his soul for naught, and drudges in the service of the devil gratis. Swearing is void of all plea, it is not the native offspring of the soul, nor interwoven with the texture of the body, nor any how allied to our frame. For, as Tillotson expresses it, 'Though some men pour out oaths as if they were natural, yet no man was ever born of a swearing constitution.' But it is a custom, a low and paltry custom, picked up by low and paltry spirits who have no sense of honor, no regard to decency, but are forced to substitute some rhapsody of nonsense to supply the vacancy of good sense. Hence the silliness of the practice can only be equalled by the silliness of those who adopt it."

It is exceedingly rude, nothing in fact can be more so, to talk to any one person in the presence of others, in a language not understood save by the two persons using it—unless you are addressing a foreigner in his own tongue, and then others should be made aware of the subject discussed. Nothing can be in worse taste than to speak in an unknown tongue, to laugh and joke in a language which leaves the rest of the company in ignorance whether they themselves may not be the subjects of your remarks or mirth.

Never hold your companion, in a conversation, by the buttonhole. If you are obliged to detain him forcibly in order to say what you wish, you are pressing upon him what is disagreeable or unwelcome, and you commit a gross breach of etiquette in so doing.

To speak to one person in a company in ambiguons terms, understood by him alone, as "G——, I saw Mr. H., to-day, and delivered your message," is as rude as if you went up to G—— and whispered in his ear.

Do not interlard your conversation with scraps of foreign language. It is an affectation of knowledge in one direction, and a sort of tacit admission of ignorance in another; for it would seem to show that the speaker was not well enough acquainted with his own language to be able to express by its aid that which could really be told as well, perhaps better, by it than any other. There are certain expressions, chiefly French, which have become domesticated in the English language, and which may occasionally be employed, but only when they come in very aptly; the constant or extended use of them is intolerable in good society.

Quotations are to be avoided as much as possible. When made, they should be exceedingly short. There can scarcely be a greater annoyance to a company than for one person to take up all the time and attention by reciting a poem, a speech, a passage from a book, especially if it be the speaker's own book, speech or poem. Of course, if the company meet especially for mutual enjoyment in elocution or recitation, this rule does not apply. It is applicable only for general society. Short, pungent, epigrammatic quotations, if suitable to the subject of conversation, may be occasionally introduced, but their use should be the exception, not the rule.

Dr. Johnson says that in order to converse well, "there must, in the first place, be knowledge—there must be materials; in the second place, there must be a command of words; in the third place, there must be imagination to place things in such views as they are not commonly seen in; and in the fourth place, there must be a presence of mind, and a resolution that is not to be overcome by failure—this last is an essential requisite; for want of it many people do not excel in conversation."

To be known as an inveterate teller of stories, is a great injury to a man in society. A short, brilliant anecdote, that is especially applicable to the conversation, known to be new and never printed, is all that a well-bred man will ever permit himself to inflict.

Remarks having, and intended to have, a double meaning—even puns—are utterly to be deprecated. It is a great liberty to appeal to the private sympathies of any one, by which I mean, to those qualities or perceptions which are, as it were, a man's private property, available for the use of his intimate friends, but not for the general public. It seems almost needless to say that under no circumstances whatever are any coarse allusions permissible

Trite remarks are simply drags upon conversation, and may produce awkward effects. It is told of Charles Lamb, that he was one day at dinner at a friend's house, where amongst a number of literary men was a solitary individual who had been invited for no apparent reason. The poor man thought that, being in such company, it behoved him to talk of some one or something literary. In an evil moment he said, without being conscious of the triteness of his remark: "Do you not think, sir, that Milton was a great genius?" Charles Lamb gazed at him curiously, rose, went to the sideboard and lighted a candle, with which he advanced, in solemn wise, to where the trite talker sat, and said as one who is about to look at some unusual object of interest—holding his candle near the poor man's head the while: "Will you allow me to examine this gentleman's pericranium?" Lamb was undoubtedly rude, but the other gave him enormous provocation.

Political and religious topics are not in good taste in general conversation. It is almost impossible to avoid strong personal feeling when a difference of opinion arises, and such discussions almost invariably lead to more warmth of expression and violence of argument than are compatible with the requirements of polite conversation.

To listen with interest and attention is as important in polite society as to converse well, and it is in the character of listener that the elegant refinement of a man accustomed to society will soonest prove itself. No matters how "flat, stale and unprofitable," the remarks of another may be, the well-bred man will listen with an appearance at least of interest, replying in such a manner as to show that he entirely "follows the thread of the discourse."

Avoid as much as possible all egotism; in conversation stick closely to Cardinal Wolsey's direction to "love thyself last." It is, to say the least of it, unseemly for a man to be constantly making himself the subject of conversation. At times it lays a man open to the attacks which his style certainly invites—as was the case with the egotist who dared to talk much of himself in the presence of Dr. Johnson, whom he had greatly irritated by his conceited talk. The doctor availed himself of an opportunity to crush him.

"Oh, indeed, I did not know that!" exclaimed the man, upon some intelligent remark made by one of the company, whereupon the doctor broke in with: "Sir, what *you* do not know would fill a very large library."

There used to be a joke against Lord Erskine, who was notably a talker of himself, that the printer, having to print a speech which his lordship had delivered, sent word to say that "he was very sorry, but he had no more 'I's' in his founts than would suffice to set up half the speech."

The subject of conversation and the method of handling it should be so ordered as not to offend either directly or indirectly.

Suitable subjects, for time and place, form an important consideration in polite conversation. Grave tones and important consideration are not suited for the chit-chat of a brief call or a social evening, nor is small talk an appropriate introduction, when the meetings are for the purpose of discussing serious matters. Let gayety or gravity rule as place and occasion demand.

Gesticulations are in excessively bad taste. If you do not wish to attract censorious remark, converse quietly and without gesture. Declamation is not conversation.

Refrain from the use of satire, even if you are master of the art. It is permissible only as a guard against impertinence, or for the purpose of checking personalities, or troublesome intrusions. Under no circumstances whatever should it be used merely for amusement's sake, to produce an effect, or in order to show off one's own wit. It must never be employed by a gentleman against a lady, though ladies are prone to indulge in the use of this wordy weapon. Their acknowledged position should, in the eyes of a true gentleman, shield them from all shafts of satire. If they, on the other hand, choose to indulge in satire, it is the part of a gentleman to remonstrate gently, and if the invective be continued, to withdraw. There was a case in point during the Austro-Prussian war. The Grand Duchess of ———, being visited by a Prussian General on business, took occasion to pour forth upon him the unmeasured violence of her temper, which had naturally enough been disturbed by the success that had attended the Prussian arms, and had been at the same time so injurious to her husband's interests. The Prussian General remonstrated, at first mildly; the invective still flowed, when the General said he would not have believed that a Prussian officer could have been called upon to endure such abuse from the lips of a high-born lady. Still the

Grand Duchess continuing to ignore the object of the General's visit, and continuing also to pour forth the bitterness of her spirit upon him, the soldier withdrew, not returning railing for railing, but simply declaring that the language used towards him was absolutely intolerable.

Do not attempt to speak with the mouth full.

Do not, however much you may be pleased with any remark, cry out "Bravo!" clap you hands, or permit any gesture, silent or otherwise, to mark your appreciation of it. A quiet expression of pleasure, or the smiling lip will show quite as plainly your sense of the wit, or fitness of the remark.

If you are flattered, repel it by quiet gravity. You cannot accept it without also accepting the contempt of the person who offers it. Refrain, too, from expressions of flattery to others; you will surely offend any hearer who has delicacy of feeling and refinement.

If an error in language, either in pronunciation or grammar, escapes those with whom you are conversing, never show that you notice it. To take occasion to repeat correctly the same word or phrase, is ill-bred in the extreme, and as much so to correct it when spoken.

In addressing any one and in general conversation, it will be well to bear in mind the advice of Polonius to his son Laertes: "Be thou familiar, but by no means vulgar;" but unless you have special reason, do not too closely adhere to his precept, "Give every man thine ear, but not thy tongue." This will only serve to make you appear reserved and reticent, when to be so would be not only out of place, but ill-bred. In society, a man should make himself as agreeable as he can, doing his best to assist conversation, as well by talking gracefully and easily, as by listening patiently, even though it be to a twice-told tale.

Do not whistle, loll about, scratch your head, or fidget with any portion of your dress while speaking. 'Tis excessively awkward, and indicative of low-breeding.

Strictly avoid anything approaching to absence of mind. There can be nothing more offensive than a pre-occupied vacant expression, an evident abstraction of self at the very time you are supposed to be listening attentively to all that is being said to you. Lord Chesterfield said: "When I see a man absent in mind, I choose to be absent in body." And there was really much reason in the remark.

Whispering is atrocious, and cannot be tolerated. It is almost as bad to endeavor to draw one person from a general conversation into a *tête a tête* discussion. Private affairs must be delayed for private interviews.

If, however, you find others have been guilty of this breach of etiquette, and you are so placed as to overhear what is intended to be a secret communication, you may with perfect propriety change your seat, or if this is not practicable, inform the persons so conversing, that their voices are audible to you.

Unless you are actually afflicted with deafness, never ask to have a sentence repeated. It implies a wandering attention. If your hearing is defective, say so, and your companion will raise his voice.

Never interrupt a speaker. It is equally rude to supply words over which your companion may hesitate a moment. Do not be guilty of a rough comment on what has been said, by such remarks as, " Yes, you *mean* so-and-so." If you understand such to be the meaning of a remark, act or answer accordingly; if you are uncertain, try to find out in some way that will not wound the feelings of the speaker.

In general conversation avoid argument. It is too engrossing of attention, and is moreover apt to break in upon the harmony of the company. If obliged to discuss a point, do so with suavity, contradicting, if necessary, with extreme courtesy, and if you see no prospect of agreement, finishing off with some happy good-natured remark to prove that you are not hurt or offended.

When addressing a person, look in his or her face, not staringly, but frankly, never fixing your eyes on the carpet or your boots.

Speak clearly and distinctly, never mumbling your words, and while avoiding a shouting tone, speak loudly enough to ensure your remarks being heard. A very low tone of voice will be heard if the words are clearly articulated and spoken slowly enough for perfect distinctness, and is much more agreeable than hurried, garbled speech loudly uttered.

Do not sit too close to your companion in conversation, and avoid any appearance of wishing secrecy.

Loud laughing and giggling are in excessively bad taste. Do not interrupt yourself by laughing at what you are about to say.

Eschew scandal, for "in scandal as in robbery, the receiver is always thought as bad as the thief." Mimicry is the lowest and most ill-bred of all buffoonery.

Swearing, sneering, private affairs either of yourself or any other, have long ago been banished out of the conversation of well-mannered people.

Never suppose, or never appear to suppose yourself the subject of the conversation or laugh of the company.

Bashfulness is an inconvenient quality, which a great authority has stated to be "the distinguishing character of a booby."

Nicknames are abominable, and are never allowed in good society. Call people and things by their right names, and avoid affectations of all kinds.

If your friends become the subject of conversation, never compare one with another, or mention the vices of one to add to the lustre of virtue of the other. Find something pleasant to say of each, that you may not earn the reputation of a backbiter.

In conversing with a foreigner, betray no impatience if he hesitates for a word to express himself, nor any ridicule if his language is faulty. If you speak his own tongue, say so when you begin the conversation, as this is never a mere display of an accomplishment, but a true kindness to "a stranger in a strange land." You are almost certain to give pleasure by so doing.

To speak constantly of public characters or distinguished people as your intimate friends, even if they are so, is a certain mark of low-breeding. Boasting of your own position, wealth, luxuries or possessions of any kind is in equally bad taste.

Never speak to a literary person of his works. You may by an apt quotation or pleasant remark show that you are familiar with them, but to question an author about his profession is ill-bred. It is equally so to speak of business matters to any man in general society. Business men do not go into the world of polite society to carry their shop, and they will not thank you for reminding them of work in their hours of relaxation.

Do not commence any conversation by the suggestion of painful or disagreeable topics. To ask a friend abruptly, "For whom are you in mourning?" may be tearing open anew a wound that was covered for the time by intercourse with society. Take other steps to satisfy yourself on this point. By the same token, do not say to a man, "That was an unfortunate affair, that failure of yours. Never, directly or indirectly, rub a sore.

Do not ask questions which relate to the private affairs of the person spoken to, and be guarded against conduct which may look like an attempt to force confidence. If too persevering in your inquiries you may be treated, and very properly, as one might treat a highwayman who sought to rob one of any other property. A man's thoughts are certainly his own most private possession, and you must be very intimate to seek to be admitted to a share in them. Even if you are so, it is far more delicate to wait until confidence is offered to you. A man has a perfect right to defend himself from cross-examination by any means, except positive falsehood.

In conversing with foreigners do not disparage any of their national customs, even if they are rude enough to attack yours. You may, pleasantly and frankly, defend the institutions of your native land, but not by comparison with the customs of other countries. If your companion is well-bred, he will admit that you possibly understand American customs better than a foreigner can do; if he is a low-bred man, no rudeness on your part will correct his manners or views.

Subjects or incidents calculated to disgust the hearers, are to be avoided in polite conversation. There is a positive fascination to some people in describing sickening or revolting scenes, but well-bred people will remember that some are sensitive upon such subjects, and all would prefer more agreeable topics.

Do not use surnames alone, even if speaking of intimate friends. For a lady to speak of her husband as "Smith" or "Jones," is vulgar in the extreme, and it is low-bred also to say "my husband," "my wife" or, except amongst relatives, to use the Christian name only, in speaking of husband or wife. Speak of your own husband or wife as, "Mr." or "Mrs. B——," and of your friends also by the surname prefix as, "Remember me to Mr. or Mrs. D."

Let no more than one person be speaking at one time.

Ridicule and personal joking cannot be too severely censured.

Avoid an officious offer of advice or your own opinion, and if you do give an opinion, be sure it is given as such and not as a fact.

If you would preserve a character for truthfulness, avoid the too common fault of exaggeration.

When visiting, be careful that you do not appear to undervalue anything around you by comparing it with what you have at home.

Beware of personal abuse or invective. Remember what Shakespeare put into the month of Cardinal Wolsey, when the Earl of Surrey said to him on his disgrace:

> "Now if you can blush and cry 'guilty' Cardinal,
> You'll show a little honesty."

Mark the proud dignity of the prelate's reply:

> "Speak on, sir;
> I dare your worst objections: If I blush
> It is to see a nobleman want manners."

Punning is a vulgarism that should be scrupulously avoided. An inveterate punster, though his play upon words may rise to the keenest wit, is yet an insufferable bore. No one feels secure in his society, or can guess what word may be torn out of a serious or brilliant remark to be tortured into a vulgar witticism, out of place and uncalled for.

Proverbs are not in good taste when introduced into conversation.

Scriptural phrases are apt to subject the speaker to a suspicion of insincerity, and should be used very seldom, and with the utmost reverence.

Cant is simply detestable.

Religion is a subject too apt to lead to long arguments if not to positive altercation to be the subject of general conversation.

Repartee is not a weapon for every-day use. There are few who can wield this polished blade skillfully, and when clumsy hands grasp it, it will wound both speaker and hearer.

The talented author of "Good Society," says:

"The great secret of talking well is to adapt your conversation as skillfully as may be to your company. Some men make a point of talking commonplace to all ladies alike, as if a woman could only be a trifler. Others, on the contrary, seem to forget in what respects the education of a lady differs from that of a gentleman, and commit the opposite error of conversing on topics with which ladies are seldom acquainted. A woman of sense has as much right to be annoyed by the one, as a lady of ordinary education by the other. You cannot pay a finer compliment to a woman of refinement and *esprit*, than by leading the conversation into such a channel as may mark your appreciation of her superior attainments.

"It should be remembered that people take more interest in their own affairs than in anything else which you can name. In *tête a tête* conversations, therefore, lead a mother to talk of her children, a young lady of her last ball, an author of his forthcoming book, or an artist of his exhibition picture. Having furnished the topic, you need only listen ; and you are thought not only agreeable, but thoroughly sensible, amiable and well-informed.

"Be careful, on the other hand, not always to make a point of talking to persons upon general matters relating to their professions. To show an interest in their immediate concerns is flattering, but to converse with them too much about their own art or profession, looks as if you thought them ignorant of other topics.

"Remember in conversation that a voice 'gentle and low' is, above all other extraneous accomplishments, an 'excellent thing in woman.' There is a certain distinct but subdued tone of voice which is peculiar to persons only of the best breeding. It is better to err by the use of too low than too loud a tone. Loud laughter is extremely objectionable in society.

"Conversation is a reflex of character. The pretentious, the illiterate, the impatient, the curious, will as inevitably betray their idiosyncrasies as the modest, the even tempered and the generous. Strive as we may, we cannot always be acting. Let us, therefore, cultivate a tone of mind, and a habit of life, the betrayal of which need not put us to shame in the company of the pure and wise, and the rest will be easy. If we make ourselves worthy of refined and intelligent society, we shall not be rejected from it; and in such society we shall acquire by example all that we have failed to learn from precept."

If you are conversing, when interrupted by a visitor, and, after the customary greetings, resume the conversation, you must recapitulate the substance of it for the benefit of the new comer.

To invariably commence a conversation by remarks on the weather shows a poverty of ideas that is truly pitiable.

Do not constantly repeat the name of a person with whom you are conversing.

A person who has travelled will probably be severely ridiculed if constantly referring to "the winter I spent in Florence," or "when I was in London."

If conversation takes a tone that is offensive to good taste, charity or justice, be silent.

Do not be too ready to correct any statement you may deem untrue. You may be yourself mistaken.

INVITATIONS.

All invitations, excepting dinner invitations, are issued in the name of the lady of the house alone. Dinner invitations are issued in the name of the gentleman and lady of the house, or when extended to gentlemen only, in the name of the host alone.

Answers to invitations, excepting such dinner invitations as are issued in the name of the gentleman only, must be addressed to the lady of the house.

When invitations are issued in the height of a fashionable season, it is best to send them out at least a fortnight beforehand. For a small company, and when gayety is not at its height, a week's notice is sufficient. For a costume ball, private theatricals or any occasion when elaborate dresses or preparations are needed, a month should be given.

Printed cards of invitation are not *en régle*, excepting for public occasions. A small note paper is the only appropriate one, and may have the initial letter or monogram stamped upon it, and the envelope. Any more fanciful decoration is in excessively bad taste.

The proper form for a dinner invitation is:

"Mr. and Mrs. G—— request the favor of Mr. and Mrs. L——'s company at dinner, on Tuesday, the 8th of January, at 5 o'clock."

Or,

"Mr. G—— requests the pleasure of Mr. L——'s company at dinner, on Tuesday, the 8th of January, at 5 o'clock."

The answer accepting the invitation should run as follows:

"Mr. and Mrs. L—— have much pleasure in accepting Mr. and Mrs. G——'s kind invitation to dinner on the 8th of January."

If declined, the following form must be used:

"Mr. and Mrs. L—— regret that a prior engagement (or other reason stated) will prevent their accepting Mr. and Mrs. G——'s kind invitation to dinner on the 8th of January."

Should the invitation be declined, some reason for the refusal must be given, and, unless an excuse (which always savors more or less of the untruthful) be wanted, it is the truest politeness to assign the cause which actually is the preventive. Whatever the cause—sickness, domestic trouble, business or any other—it should be stated as concisely as possible in the answer, which in any case should be dispatched as soon as possible (certainly the next day) after the receipt of the invitation, that the hostess may have time to summon other guests in the stead of those declining her first invitations.

After an invitation is once accepted, it should be scrupulously observed. Nothing but the most absolute necessity should prevent you from going, and when such necessity arises, it should be communicated directly, with a full explanation of the preventing cause even if it is within half an hour of the appointed dinner time. If earlier, send the explanation as soon as possible.

Invitations to dinner and the answers must be sent by a special messenger. The post is proverbially uncertain, and the non-arrival of an expected invitation or its answer, may cause lasting offence.

It is a breach of etiquette, to say nothing of practical inconvenience, to bring an unassorted company together at dinner. Great people, public characters, literary celebrities or distinguished guests from any cause should not be invited merely because they are such. They will be uncomfortable if the guests summoned to meet them are not congenial, and the remainder of your company equally so. No one guest should be too conspicuous. A harmonious blending of tastes and qualities should be the object in view. Persons moving in one circle of society should not, as a general rule, be invited to meet those who move in another circle. A man of strong political bias in one direction, should not be invited to meet a party opposed to his views; persons of known and marked differences in religious matters should not be invited to meet each other, and above all, avoid the social collision of those whom you know to be personal enemies. The best guide in such matters is common sense, coupled with a little judicious forethought.

Invitations to large balls should be sent out at least a fortnight before the time appointed, and are worded thus:

"Mrs. L——'s compliments to Miss G——, and requests the pleasure of her company at a ball, on Wednesday, the 7th of March, at 9 o'clock."

The answer is as follows:

"Miss G——'s compliments to Mrs. L——, and accepts with pleasure her kind invitation for Wednesday, March 7th."

Or,

"Miss G—— regrets a recent death in her family will prevent her accepting Mrs. L——'s kind invitation for March 7th."

An invitation to an evening party is worded:

"Mrs. S—— compliments to Mr. and Mrs. T——, and requests the pleasure of their company on March 9th, at 8 o'clock."

Such an invitation calls for full evening dress. The answer is the same as for a ball invitation.

Invitations to pic-nics, private theatricals, concerts, tea parties and other entertainments, generally state the nature of such entertainment, and are a little less formal than those already given.

For a musical party:

"Mrs. R—— requests the pleasure of Mr. and Mrs. P——'s company, on Thusday evening, Feb. 10th, at 8'clock, to meet the members of the Harmonia Musical Society."

And if you have a programme of the concert, enclose it.

Or,

"Mrs. F—— expects a few friends on Monday evening next, at 8 o'clock, to take part in some dramatic readings, and would be happy to have Miss B—— join the party."

Or,

"Mrs. S——'s compliments to Miss P——, and would be pleased to have her join a pic-nic party to Pine Grove, on Wednesday, June 14th. Carriages start from Mrs. S——'s at 9 o'clock, and a place will be reserved for Miss P——."

Notes of invitation must always be dated, and your address in full written in one corner, thus:

"Feb. 6th, 18—.

"Miss M—— requests the pleasure of Miss N——'s company to a small evening party, on Friday evening next, at 8 o'clock.

"No. 762 R—— Street."

The body of the invitation must be in the middle of the sheet, and date a little above to the right, the address a little below to the left.

The envelopes containing invitations must be directed always to the private residence of the person invited, never to a place of business or office.

When the officers of a regiment or a ship are invited to an entertainment, and it is not possible to invite them all, it is customary to send an invitation to the Colonel or Commander, accompanied by a certain number of blank tickets, if it be a public ball, or by an intimation that the host would be glad to see Colonel or Captain ——— and so many of the officers of the regiment or ship.

Invitations by a regiment to a ball, to be given by the officers, are worded as follows:

"Col. ——— and the officers of the —— Regiment, U. S. I. (or other branch of the service), request the pleasure of Mr. and Mrs. C———'s company on the 7th of December, at 9 o'clock.

"R——— Barracks, corner of ——— and ——— Streets."

Answers should be addressed to the Colonel of the regiment, and worded thus:

"Mr. and Mrs. C———'s compliments to Colonel ——— and the officers of the —— Regiment, U. S. I., and accept with pleasure their polite invitation for the 7th of December."

In case an officer desires to invite his personal friends, he encloses his own card in the invitation, but these must all be issued in the form already given, the card explaining to which officer the compliment is to be attributed.

Invitations to a Naval ball are issued in the name of the "Captain and officers of the U. S. Ship ———," or simply in the name of "The Officers of the U. S. Ship ———."

On the corner of the card the name of the officer to whom the answers are to be sent, should be written.

An officer of higher rank, or a public official of high position, will signify on his card what aide-de-camp or clerk is to receive the answers to his invitations, and will issue them in the joint name of himself and wife, thus:

"General and Mrs. E——— request the pleasure of Mr. and Mrs. D———'s company, on Thursday, the 6th of November, at 8 o'clock.

"Direct answers to Capt. E. C———."

Verbal invitations are given only when the occasion is a very informal one, and imply plain dress, early hours and a small company.

Invitations to concerts, theatre or opera, should be sent in time to secure good seats, if accepted. The usual style is:

"Mr. G—— would be much pleased to have Mrs. and Miss Hunt's company at the opera, on Wednesday evening, when La Trovatore will be performed by the Italian troupe at the Academy of Music."

Such an invitation calls for an immediate answer from the elder lady, and should be as follows:

"Mrs. and Miss Hunt accept with pleasure Mr. G——'s polite invitation to listen to a favorite opera on Wednesday evening."

Or if declined:

"Mrs. Hunt regrets that a prior engagement will prevent her own and Miss Hunt's acceptance of Mr. G——'s polite invitation for Wednesday evening."

For a general reception, invitations are printed upon cards, thus:

Mrs. Williams,
AT HOME,
Wednesday Evening, January 14th,
No. 348 —— STREET.

Such cards do not require any answer.

DINNER COMPANY.

On no occasion is a want of punctuality more ill-bred than at a dinner party, whether it is the guests who are late, or the hostess who allows dinner to be later than the time appointed. Boileau remarks, with as much truth as sarcasm:

"I have always been punctual to the hour of dinner, for I know that those whom I kept waiting would employ those unpleasant moments to sum up all my faults."

To arrive too early is to annoy the lady of the house by disturbing her at her toilet.

To arrive too late is injurious to the dinner, to the temper of your host, of the other guests and of the servants.

It is really a sad breach of etiquette to be later than the hour named in your invitation for dinner, and from ten to fifteen minutes before it is quite soon enough for your arrival.

As regards the hour for dinner, etiquette, strictly so called, has not prescribed anything. Custom, the fashion, convenience, a score of things may control it. From five to eight o'clock, according somewhat to the season of the year, is the present fashionable limit. By that time the business of most men is over for the day, which can scarcely be said of an hour earlier than five.

The lady of the house should be in her drawing-room, ready to receive her guests, ten or fifteen minutes before the hour fixed for their arrival, and the daughters of the house should be with her, and not drop in one by one after the guests' arrival. The gentleman of the house should also be present, and in case it is a strictly gentleman's party, at which no hostess presides, he must be all ready before the appointed time to do the honors.

On guests being announced, the lady advances a few steps towards them, and should receive them cordially with some words of welcome.

The hostess must never betray any chagrin at the lateness of a guest, but try to place the unfortunate last arrival as much at ease as possible by her cordial welcome and unembarrassed manner.

Before all the guests have arrived the lady should have made her arrangements as to what gentleman and lady are to go in to dinner together, and before dinner is announced the gentlemen of the party should be informed what lady they are to escort to the table.

The gentleman of the house offers his arm to the lady most honored amongst the guests, the gentleman most distinguished offers his arm to the lady of the house.

Gentlemen give the left arm to a lady, excepting military officers in full dress, who give the right arm, as the sword is inconveniently worn for offering the left. In all other cases the right arm must be left free.

The order of procession being settled, the company move according to it from the drawing-room to the dining-room, as soon as dinner is announced.

The host sits at the bottom of the table, the hostess at the top. At the right of the host is placed the lady he escorted from the drawing-room, and at the right of the hostess her escort. The next place of honor is at the left of the hostess.

It is a good plan, and rapidly becoming an established custom, to have small cards with the names of the guests written upon them, laid upon the plate at each seat. Each one thus taking the place assigned prevents confusion, and gives the hostess the privilege of placing near to each other the guests who will prove mutually agreeable.

Gentlemen should stand behind their respective chairs until all the ladies are seated, and then take their own seats, being careful that their chairs do not stand upon the dresses of the ladies beside them.

Seats having been apportioned to all, grace is said, by a clergyman if there is one present, if not, by the host. The clergyman should be invited to say grace by the host.

If the dinner is *a la Russe*, there will not be any carving done on the table itself.

If the party is small, mere *en famille*, the hostess will have a dish before her, the contents of which will have to be carved. The gentleman on her right hand should in that case offer to carve for her, but if she declines, should not press the offer. Many ladies are excellent carvers, and like to appear so.

There is no space in our little volume for directions upon carving, nor do they form any portion of the art of etiquette. All that etiquette has to say on the subject is that you must not stand up to carve; you must not pursue the bird, joint or whatever the meat may be, all round the dish; nor should you comment upon the age of the fowl, the toughness of the meat or your own awkwardness in carving. If you really do not understand it, do not attempt it; say so and let the waiter cut it up.

Never be helped twice to soup or fish, and indeed it appears low-bred to be twice served to any one dish. You may refuse either soup or fish, but make no comment if you do, as to your liking or dislike for the dish, nor is it incumbent upon you to state that "soup does not agree with you," or that "fish always make you ill;" any such remarks are rude. Simply to say "no, thank you," in refusing a dish, is all the reply that strict etiquette will allow upon the subject.

No remarks should be made by the host or hostess on the refusal of a guest to partake of a proffered dish. Pressing the food upon a guest with "Oh, do take some," or "You must, it was made by so-and-so," or indeed any remark upon the repast, is not only annoying to the guest, but a proof of low-breeding in the entertainers. There is a sort of hospitality about it, but it is a rough barbarism. Who does not remember the description of Bridget Elias' hospitable *gaucherie* in Charles Lamb's "Poor Relation," when urging the poor relation to eat with the speech: "Do take some more; remember you do not get pudding every day."

Never should a host or hostess apologize for the fare set before their guest. Such apologies are generally a mere fishing for compliment, untrue and in entirely bad taste. In inviting his friends to dinner, the host binds himself to set before them the best his house and purse can afford, and if the fare is good the guest will soon find it out, if bad, no apologies will make it any better.

It is in bad taste to apologize to the waiters for the trouble given them, and betrays a lamentable ignorance of the customs of society. They are hired to wait upon the guests, and it is no affair of those guests how they feel, as long as they discharge their duty. To reprove a waiter is the height of ill-breeding.

Do not, when a dish is brought to you, say you prefer to be helped after some one else. Accept or refuse what is offered to you, and let the waiter pass the dish on. A gentleman, however, will see that the lady he has escorted to the table is helped as she wishes, before he attends to his own dinner, but to interfere with the lady on the other side of him is an insult to *her* escort. He may ask the lady under his care if she will be helped from any dish offered him, before he accepts or declines for himself, and will issue her orders for her to the waiter when she selects her dinner.

A gentleman or a lady will always say " Thank you " to a waiter, but nothing more.

A guest must never find fault with any dish placed before him, and to appear to question the quality or freshness of the viands by smelling or fastidiously tasting them, is a positive insult to the gentleman who has invited him to his table.

A host or hostess may never find fault before their guests, neither with the dinner, with the servants, nor with each other. Burnt soup, fish boiled to rags, underdone vegetables, heavy pastry, must be endured with smiling equanimity. No scowl must greet the crash that announces the fall of a tray of the finest glass, no word of remonstrance greet the deluge of a plate of soup over the table-cloth. If care has not been taken to secure first-rate cooks and well-trained waiters, the faults of omission and commission must be endured with placid serenity.

After the ladies have all been served, the guests to the right of the hostess must be attended to, then the guest on her left, and so on until all are served. Ten persons are all that one cook can properly prepare a dinner for, and three waiters will be amply employed in waiting upon that number. If more are invited the attempt to make the conversation general had better not be made, but the guests allowed to converse *tête a tête.*

Wine should be handed by the waiters after soup. To decline wine by covering the mouth of the wine-glass with the hand is an ill-bred gesture. Say simply "Not any, thank you," and the waiter will not fill your glass.

Fish follows next in order. A slice, neatly *cut,* not hashed up by bad carving, should be placed upon each plate, with a slice of egg, and fish sauce. If there be a silver knife, use it to cut the fish. If not, take your fork in your right hand and supply the place of the knife by a small piece of bread, which you should cut off, and when your fish is eaten, leave upon your plate.

Do not eat as if you had good fare for the first time in your life —that is to say, do not eat ravenously, and do not eat in a noticeable way.

Never smack the lips when eating.

Never take a long, deep breath after you finish eating, as if the exercise had fatigued you.

Never make noises in your mouth or throat.

Never suck your teeth, or pass your tongue round the outside of your gums.

Never, even with cheese, put your knife into your mouth.

Never pick your teeth, or put your finger into your mouth.

If you find you have a fish-bone in your mouth, cover your lips with a napkin to remove it. It is better to be very careful to remove all bones before putting fish into your mouth. On no account spit the bones out upon your plate.

Never take the bones of fowl or birds up in your fingers to gnaw or suck them. Remove the meat with your knife, and convey it to your mouth with your fork, never being too eager to clean off every particle of flesh.

Wipe your finger tips, if soiled, upon the table napkin, never upon your tongue or the table-cloth. An elegant eater will never have occasion to think of his fingers.

Never use the table-cloth to wipe your mouth, you might as well use it in place of your pocket handkerchief.

Never remark upon what is placed before you, either in praise or dispraise of it.

Neither drink nor speak when you have anything in your mouth.

When you are helped, begin to eat, without regard to those who have already, or have not yet, been helped.

Never watch the dishes as they are uncovered, nor make any exclamation when you see their contents.

Under no circumstances tuck your napkin, bib-fashion, into your shirt collar. Unfold it partially and put it in your lap, covering your knees. A lady may slip a corner under her belt if there is danger of its slipping upon her dress, but a gentleman must be awkward indeed if he lets his napkin fall upon the floor.

No gentleman will ever settle himself in his chair, pushing back his cuffs, as if for a "set-to," at the table.

If you make any general remark, do not look up at the waiters to see what effect it has upon them. If they are well-trained they will not move a muscle at hearing the most laughable story, nor will they give any sign whatever that they have not closed their ears like deaf adders to all that has been going on. In any case, however, you must refrain from noticing them.

If you want anything, take the occasion of a waiter being near to you, to ask for it in an undertone. To shout out "Waiter!" or order one about, as if you were in a restaurant, is a certain mark of ill-breeding.

Unless the party is a very small one, general conversation is impossible. In such a case, you must converse with those on either side of you, not confining your remarks exclusively to one.

Talk in a low, quiet tone, but never in a whisper.

To affect an air of mystery or secrecy at a dinner-table, is an insult to your companion and company assembled.

It is in bad taste to force the attention of the company upon yourself by loud talking or loud laughing.

Too many jokes or anecdotes are in bad taste, but the subjects for conversation should not be too serious.

Any gentleman propounding a conundrum at the dinner-table, deserves to be taken away by the police.

To use one's own knife, spoon or fingers, instead of the butter-knife, sugar-tongs or salt-spoons, is to persuade the company that you have never seen the latter articles before, and are unacquainted with their use.

Never eat all that is on your plate, and above all never be guilty of the *gaucherie* of scraping your plate, or passing your bread over it as if to clean it.

Never fill your mouth so full that you cannot converse; at the same time avoid the appearance of merely playing with your food. Eat in small mouthfuls, and rather slowly than rapidly.

If upon opening fruit you find it is not perfect, or there is a worm in it, pass your plate quietly and without remark to the waiter, who will bring you a clean one.

None but a low-bred clown will ever carry fruit or *bon bons* away from the table.

Drinking wine with people is an old custom, but it will now-a-days be found to exist only among the past or passing generation. If you are, however, asked to take wine with any one, you should fill your glass with the same sort of wine your friend has, and raise it to your lips. You need only taste, not act upon the principle of "no heel-taps."

A man would be looked upon as a curiosity, nay, many would not understand what he meant, who should at the present day propose a "sentiment" before drinking wine.

Never spit from your mouth the skins of grapes, the stones or pips of fruits. Receive them upon the prongs of your fork, laid horizontally, and place them as conveniently as so inelegant a process will allow upon the edge of your plate.

Never play with your fingers upon the table.

Never play with your knife and fork, fidget with your salt-cellar, balance your spoon on your tumbler, make pills of your bread, or perform any of those vulgar antics unfortunately too often seen at table.

Never in conversation, illustrate your remarks by plans drawn upon the table-cloth with your nail, or built of your knife, fork and spoon.

Never stretch your feet out under the table, so as to touch those of your opposite neighbor. It is quite as bad to put them up under you upon the chair-bar, or curl them up under the chair itself.

Try to take an easy position at table, neither pressing closely up to it, nor yet so far away as to risk depositing your food upon the floor instead of conveying it to your mouth.

Never touch fruit with your fingers. If you wish to peel an apple, a pear or a peach, hold the fruit on a fork in your left hand, and peel with a silver knife in your right. Eat it in small slices cut from the whole fruit, but never bite it, or anything else at table. Need I say no fruit should ever be sucked at the table.

When the hostess thinks her lady friends have taken as much dessert as they wish, she catches the eye of the principal among them; an interchange of ocular telegraphing takes place, the hostess rises, and with her all the company rise; the gentlemen make a passage for the ladies to pass; the one who is nearest to the door opens it, and holds it open until all the ladies have passed out of the room.

As soon as the ladies have retired the gentlemen may resume their seats for more wine and conversation, but it is a very poor compliment to the lady guests to linger long in the dining-room.

The ladies upon leaving the dining-room, retire to the drawing-room, and occupy themselves until the gentlemen again join them. It is well for the hostess to have a reserve force for this interval, of photographic albums, stereoscopes, annuals, new music, in fact, all the ammunition she can provide to make this often tedious interval pass pleasantly.

If you dine in the French fashion, the gentlemen rise with the ladies, each offering his arm to the lady he escorted to dinner, and all proceed to the drawing-room together.

If the gentlemen remain to have coffee served in the dining-room, tea may be served in the drawing-room to the ladies.

Upon returning to the drawing-room the gentlemen should never cluster round the door, but join the ladies at once, striving to repay the hospitality of the hostess by making themselves as agreeable as possible to the guests.

From two to three hours after dinner is the proper time to leave the house.

If the dinner is for the gentlemen guests alone, and the lady of house presides, her duties are over when she rises after dessert. The gentlemen do not expect to find her in the drawing-room again. In this case cigars may be served with the coffee, and then the servants may retire, unless especially summoned to wait. If smoking is indulged in, have placed upon the table a number of small match boxes, ashes receivers, and between the chairs spittoons. And here let me add a few words upon smoking taking from an English authority, but which, with a few exceptions will apply equally well to lovers of the weed upon this side of the water. He says:

"But what shall I say of the fragrant weed which Raleigh taught our gallants to puff in capacious bowls; which a royal pedant denounced in a famous 'Counterblast,' which his flattering laureate, Ben Jonson, ridiculed to please his master; which our wives and sisters protest gives rise to the dirtiest and most unsociable habit a man can indulge in; of which some fair favorers declare that they love the smell, and others that they will never marry an indulger (which, by the way, they generally end in doing); which has won a fame over more space and among better men than Noah's grape has ever done; which doctors still dispute about, and boys get sick over; but which is the solace of the weary laborer; the support of the ill-fed; the refresher of overwrought brains; the soother of angry fancies; the boast of the exquisite; the excuse of the idle; the companion of the philosopher; and the tenth muse of the poet. I will go neither into the the medical nor the moral questions about the dreamy calming cloud. I will content myself so far with saying what may be said for everything that can bless and curse mankind, that in moderation it is at least harmless; but what is moderate and what is not, must be determined in each individual case, according to the habits and constitution of the subjects. If it cures asthma, it may destroy digestion; if it soothes the nerves, it may, in excess, produce a chronic irritability.

"But I will regard it in a social point of view, and, first as a narcotic, notice its effects on the individual character. I believe then, that in moderation it diminishes the violence of the passions, and particularly that of the temper. Interested in the subject, I have taken care to seek instances of members of the same family having the same violent temper by inheritance, of whom the one has been calmed down by smoking, and the other gone on in his passionate course. I believe that it induces a habit of calm reflectiveness, which causes us to take less prejudiced, perhaps less zealous views of life, and to be therefore less irritable in our converse with our fellow-creatures. I am inclined to think that the clergy, the squirearchy and the peasantry, are the most prejudiced and most violent classes in this country (England); there may be other reasons for this, but it is noteworthy that these are the classes which smoke least. On the other hand, I confess that it induces a certain lassitude, and a lounging, easy mode of life, which is fatal both to the precision of manners and the vivacity of conversation. The mind of a smoker is contemplative rather than active, and if the weed cures our irritability, it kills our wit. I believe that it is a fallacy to suppose that it encourages drinking. There is more drinking and less smoking in England than in any other country of the the civilized world. There was more drinking among the gentry of last century, who never smoked at all. Smoke and wine do not go well together. Coffee and beer are its best accompaniments; and the one cannot intoxicate, the other must be largely imbibed to do so. I have observed among young bachelors that very little wine is drunk in their chambers, and that beer is gradually taking its place. The cigar, too, is an excuse for rising from the dinner-table, where there are no ladies to go to.

"In another point of view, I am inclined to think that smoking has conduced to make the society of men, when alone, less riotous, less quarrelsome and even less vicious than it was. Where young men now blow a common cloud, they were formerly driven to a fearful consumption of wine; and this in their heads, they were ready and roused to any iniquity. But the pipe is the bachelor's wife. With it, he can endure solitude longer, and is not forced into low society in order to shun it. With it, too, the idle can pass many an hour, which otherwise he would have given, not to work, but to extravagant follies. With it, he is no longer restless, and impatient for excitement of any kind. We never hear now of young blades issuing in bands from their wine to beat the watch or disturb the slumbering citizens, as we did thirty or forty years ago, when smoking was still a rarity; they are all puffing harmlessly in their chambers now. But, on the other hand, I foresee with dread a too tender allegiance to the pipe, to the destruction of good society, and the abandonment of the ladies. No wonder they hate it, dear creatures! the pipe is the worst rival a woman can have, and it is one whose eyes she cannot scratch out; who improves with age, while she herself declines; who has an art which no woman possesses, that of never wearying her devotee; who is silent, yet a companion; costs little, yet gives much pleasure; who, lastly, never upbraids, and always yields the same joy. Ah! this is a powerful rival to wife or maid; and no wonder that at last the woman succumbs, consents, and, rather than lose her lord or master, even supplies the hated herb with her own fair hands.

"There are rules to limit this indulgence. One must never smoke, nor even ask to smoke, in the company of the fair. If they know that in a few minutes you will be running off to your cigar, the fair will do well—say it is in a garden, or so—to allow you to bring it out and smoke it there.

"One must never smoke, again, in the streets—that is, in daylight. The deadly crime may be committed, like burglary, after dark, but not before.

"One must never smoke in a room inhabited at times by the ladies; thus, a well-bred man, who has a wife or sister, will not offer to smoke in the dining-room after dinner.

"One must never smoke in a public place, where ladies are or might be; for instance, a flower-show or promenade.

"One may smoke in a railway-carriage, in spite of by-laws, if one has first obtained the consent of every one present; but if there be a lady there, though she give her consent, smoke not. In nine cases out of ten, she will give it from good nature.*

"One must never smoke in a close carriage; one may ask and obtain leave to smoke, when returning from a pic-nic or expedition, in an open carriage.

"One must never smoke in a theatre, on a race-course, nor in church. This last is not, perhaps, a needless caution. In the Belgian churches you see a placard announcing: '*Ici on ne mache pas du tabac.*'

"One must never smoke when anybody shows an objection to it.

"One must never smoke a pipe in the streets.

"One must never smoke at all in the coffee-room of a hotel.

"One must never smoke, without asking permission, in the presence of a clergyman.

"But if you smoke, or if you are in the company of smokers, and are to appear afterwards in the presence of ladies, you must change your clothes to smoke in. A host who invites you to smoke will generally offer you an old coat for the purpose.

"You must also after smoking rinse the mouth well out, and if possible brush the teeth.

"You should never smoke in another person's house without leave, and you should not ask leave to do so, if there are ladies in the house.

"When you are going to smoke a cigar, you should offer one at the same time to anybody present.

"You should always smoke a cigar given to you whether good or bad, and never make any remark upon its quality."

At a gentleman's party it is the host alone who may call upon any of the company for a toast, a speech or a song. No matter how much others may desire it, they may never invite each other.

* In America, cars are especially provided for smokers, and no gentleman will violate etiquette by smoking in any other.

During the week following a dinner party, it is etiquette for each guest to call upon the hostess, and it is rude to delay the call more than a fortnight.

In concluding this chapter we give from a modern English work the following bills of fare for dinners suiting the different seasons of the year, which may be useful to young housekeepers :

MENUS OF FOUR CHOICE DINNERS, ADAPTED TO EACH SEASON OF THE YEAR.

JANUARY.—(FOR TEN PERSONS.)

Consommé soup, with quenelles ; Turbot, with Dutch sauce.

TWO REMOVES.—Braized fillet of veal, larded à la Chateaubriand ; Roast turkey, with purée of mushrooms.

FOUR ENTRÉES.—Oyster Kromeskys, à la Russe ; Pork cutlets, sauce Robert ; Partridges, à la Prince of Wales ; Suprême of fowls, à la Macédoine.

SECOND COURSE.—Pintail ; Snipes.

ONE REMOVE.—Fondu of Parmesan cheese.

FOUR ENTREMÊTS.—Salad, à la Rachel ; Vol-au-vent of preserved greengages ; Plombières cream iced ; Braized celery with brown sauce.

APRIL.—(FOR EIGHT PERSONS.)

Cray-fish soup ; Spey trout, parsley sauce.

TWO REMOVES.—Boiled fowls, oyster sauce ; Glazed tongue à la jardinière.

TWO ENTRÉES.—Lamb cutlets, asparagus, peas ; Boudins of rabbits, à la Reine.

SECOND COURSE.—Lobster salad ; Green goose.

FOUR ENTREMÊTS.—Orange fritters ; Tapioca pudding ; Wine jelly ; Potatoes à la Lyonnaise.

JUNE.—(FOR TWELVE PERSONS.)

Purée of green peas, soup ; Stewed sturgeon, matelotte sauce ; Fillets of mackerel à la maitre d'hôtel.

TWO REMOVES.—Roast fore-quarter of lamb ; Spring chickens à la Montmorency.

FOUR ENTRÉES.—Fillets of ducklings, with green peas ; Mutton cutlets à la Wyndham ; Blanquette of chicken with cucumbers ; Timbale of macaroni à la Milanaise.

SECOND COURSE.—Pigeons ; Leveret.

TWO REMOVES.—Flemish gauffers ; Iced Soufflé.

SIX ENTREMÊTS.—French beans, stewed ; Mayonnaise of chicken ; Peas à la Française ; Peach jelly with noyau ; Love's wells glacé with chocolate ; Flave of apricots and rice.

OCTOBER.—(FOR EIGHT PERSONS.)

Potage à la Julienne ; Baked haddock, Italian sauce.

TWO REMOVES.—Braized neck of mutton, en cherveuil ; Roast pheasant à la Chipolata.

TWO ENTRÉES.—Pork cutlets, tomato sauce ; Curried rabbit and rice.

SECOND COURSE.—Roast black-cock ; Oyster omelette.

FOUR ENTREMÊTS. — Potatoes à la Duchesse ; Blanc mange ; Apple tartlets ; Semolina pudding.

MENU OF A FIRST RATE CHRISTMAS DINNER.

CHRISTMAS DINNER.

Turtle soup ; Turbot à la Vatel ; Fillets of sole à la Tartare.

THREE REMOVES.—Roast turkey, Périgueux sauce ; Braized ham à la jardinière ; Spiced round of beef.

FOUR ENTRÉES.— Marrow patties ; Salmi of pheasants à la financière ; Sweet breads à la Saint Cloud ; Mutton cutlets ; à la Vicomtesse.

SECOND COURSE.—Woodcocks ; Grouse ; Mince pies ; Plum pudding.

SIX ENTREMÊTS. — Brocoli with Parmesan cheese ; Italian creams ; Croûte à l'Amanas · Salad à la Rachel ; Meringues à la Parisienne ; Punch jelly.

BALLS.

The form of invitations will be found on page 49.

An invitation to a ball should be sent out from two to three weeks before the evening, and should be answered within a day or two of being received.

As to the number of guests to be invited, no precise rules can be laid down. The size of your room does not seem to be any guide. The custom is to ask rather more than twice as many as your rooms will hold; but one-third more will be enough, as it will allow of disappointments at the last moment, even if all have accepted the invitations. Besides, during the gayest of the season, the fashion of going to several balls in one night necessitates ensuring the presence of a sufficiently large number of guests all through the evening. If you really wish for dancing, do not exceed the last limits. If, however, your aim is to have the largest ball of the season, a crush and crowd, to make a sensation, then invite your entire visiting list, and endure the consequences.

A hundred guests constitute a "ball;" over that, a "large ball;" under that, merely a "dance."

One of the first requisites of a ball-room is thorough ventilation, especially if there is a prospect of a large number of guests.

One of the most desirable points in a ball is to have a beautifully-arranged room. The floor must be well waxed, and perfectly even, and it is well to draw a cord across two-thirds of it, not admitting more than can dance inside the space so cut off at once. The French make their ball-rooms perfect flower-gardens. Every comer has its immense bouquet; the walls are gracefully wreathed; bouquets, baskets, and exquisitely decorated pots of growing plants are placed in every available place. The staircases, landings, and supper-room are all filled with floral treasures, harmonizing with fine effect with the brilliant lights and gay the dresses of the ladies. It adds to the effect to conceal the musicians behind a screen of evergreen and flowers.

The dressing-rooms should be provided with two servants apiece, and small cards, with the names of the invited guests upon them, should be in readiness to pin to the wraps of each one.

In each dressing-room, have plenty of water, soap, and towels upon the washstand, several brushes and combs, small hand-mirrors, pin-cushions well filled, and stick pomade upon the bureau. The ladies' room should also have hair-pins, a work-box in readiness to repair any accidental rip or tear; cologne, hartshorn, and salts, in case of faintness. The gentlemen's room should be provided with a boot-jack, a whisk, and a clothes-brush.

No one should accept an invitation to a ball who cannot or who will not dance. They are mere encumbrances. Nothing is more trying to the feelings of a hostess than to see a number of wall-flowers ornamenting (?) her ball-room.

The hour at which one may go to a ball varies from ten o'clock in the evening until daybreak. Any one who attends several balls in one evening will, of course, find it impossible to appear at an early hour at each one.

The lady of the house—who should, if possible, know the name of everybody who enters the room—must stand near the door, so as to receive her guests, to each of whom she must find something to say, no matter how trifling. The host must also be near, to welcome arrivals, and the sons to introduce people. The young ladies must see that the dances are kept up, and should not dance themselves till they have found partners for all their friends. They may with perfect propriety ask any gentleman present to be introduced to a partner, and he is bound to accept the invitation; but the lady must be careful whom she asks. Many present may be entire strangers to her. Miss A. has brought her betrothed; Miss B. introduces her cousin, Captain ——, on a short leave of absence from his regiment in Texas; Miss C. presents her brother, just returned from California; Miss D. begs leave to introduce a cousin on a short visit to the city; Miss E., a belle, has informed a dozen or two of her admirers where they may bow to her on the evening of the ball. All these strangers bow to the hostess, and must be provided with partners. The "Man in the Club Window" says:

"I have known a case where a distinguished-looking young man, having declined the lady's invitation to dance, but being pressed by, 'I can't make up the lancers without you,' somewhat reluctantly accepted, performed his part so well that his partner was quite *éprise* with him, and even ventured on a little flirtation. You can imagine her dismay when, a little later in the evening, she saw her charming acquaintance carrying up a pile of plates from the kitchen to the supper-room. For the first time in her life, she had danced with an occasional waiter."

If a gentleman act as escort to a lady, he must call at her house, at the hour she appoints, with a carriage, and he is expected to send a bouquet in the course of the afternoon. Upon reaching the house of the hostess for the evening, he must escort his fair charge to the dressing-room, leave her at the door, make his own toilet as rapidly as possibly, and return to meet the lady at the dressing-room door again, escort her to the ball-room, and at once to the hostess. She is obliged by etiquette to dance the first dance with him; but after that, he may with propriety allow her liberty to select other partners, always watching, however, to see that she is never neglected. He must be her escort to supper, and ready at any moment to leave the ball-room to escort her home again.

If a gentleman is unaccompanied by a lady, he must invite one of the ladies of the house for the first dance, and yield gracefully if she declines on the plea of want of room or partners for all her guests, consenting smilingly if she requests him to lead out the homeliest and most awkward of her wall-flowers.

The music must be first a march, then a quadrille, a polka, a waltz, a galop, and so on, with two or three round dances to each quadrille, until fourteen dances are completed, when another march announces supper. Seven to ten dances may follow supper. Each guest must be provided with a ball-card with a printed programme of the dances, and space for the engagements upon it, and a tiny pencil attached to it. Many ladies carry their own engagement-card; but they must depend upon the programme for the order of dances. The fashion of hanging a few printed programmes in the room is not considered *en règle*.

The supper-room must be thrown open at midnight, and remain open until the ball closes. It is, however, an extreme of bad taste and low breeding for gentlemen to cluster round the table in groups and remain there. It is one of the duties of the hostess to see that no young lady loses her supper for want of an escort to the supper-room. If there are no young gentlemen in the family, she must request one of her guests to go to the rescue of the forlorn maiden.

No gentleman must wait until the music has commenced before selecting his partner.

A lady who declines dancing on the pretext of fatigue must dance no more, unless she has said she wished to rest for that dance alone.

If a lady decline dancing with a gentlemen, it is rude for him to turn from her to another lady who has heard the refusal, and invite her to dance. If the first lady has a prior engagement, he must seek another partner in another part of the room; if she refuses from fatigue or a disinclination to dance that set, it is a compliment to her for him to remain beside her, and endeavor to entertain her while the dance is in progress.

A lady should never give her bouquet, gloves, and fan to a gentleman to hold during a dance, unless he is her husband, brother, or escort for the evening.

A gentleman, in waltzing with a young lady, must never encircle her waist until the dance actually commences, and drop his arm from around her as soon as the music ceases. American gentlemen would do well to study the waltz with a German teacher, as they understand more perfectly than any others the most delicate way of dancing this objectionable dance, and, above all, how to hold a lady lightly and firmly without embracing her.

When a lady expresses a desire to sit down before the close of a dance, it is exceedingly rude for a gentlemen to insist upon a continuation of the dance. He must escort her to a seat at once, and then express his regret at the interrupted pleasure. She may with propriety release him to seek another partner, but it is a poor compliment for him to accept the proposal.

A gentleman should never invite a lady to be his partner in a dance with which he is not perfectly familiar. It is tiresome in the extreme to guide a partner through a dance, and the ballroom is not a dancing-school for practice.

If a gentleman takes a lady's seat during a dance, he must rise from it as soon as the dance is over, not waiting for her to actually return to it, as she may hesitate to do if she sees that it is occupied.

No lady must enter or cross a ball-room unescorted.

No lady may refuse to be introduced to a gentleman at a private ball; but at a public ball she may with perfect propriety refuse any introduction made by the master of ceremonies, or by mere acquaintances.

Confidential conversation in a ball-room is in extreme bad taste.

Do not be too particular about dancing. Taking steps in a quadrille is out of date, all the figures being executed to a graceful walk.

To remain too late at a ball is not well-bred, and seems to imply that you are unaccustomed to such pleasures. Do not engage yourself, therefore, for the last two or three dances.

No gentleman should take the vacant seat next to a lady unless he is acquainted with her, and not then without first asking permission.

A gentleman must offer his arm, never his hand, to lead a lady to and from the dance.

A lady must be very careful not to engage herself to two gentlemen for the same dance, unless, for a round dance, she states: "I am engaged for the first half of the waltz, but will dance the second part with you." In that case, she must tell her first partner of her second engagement, that she may not offend him when she takes another partner after leaving him.

If a lady wishes to decline dancing, whether from dislike to the gentleman who invites her, or from whatever cause, she must make some excuse; but she must never refuse point blank, nor must she, after having refused to dance with one gentleman, consent to dance with another.

When introduced, it is sufficient for a gentleman to say to a lady, "May I have the pleasure of dancing this waltz with you, Miss C——?" or if the lady be engaged for the first dance following the introduction, he may request the favor of putting his name upon her engagement card for another.

A young lady should not dance more than twice with the same gentleman, unless she wants to be noticed, or is indifferent whether she be so or not.

A lady may consult her own pleasure about recognizing a ball-room acquaintance at a future meeting.

Every gentleman must make a point of inviting the ladies of the house to dance; and if he be kind, he will certainly devote himself—for a portion of the evening, at least—to those ladies for whom the May of life has bloomed and passed away, and who generally sit round the room looking wistfully disconsolate.

After every dance following the announcement of supper, offer your partner your arm, and invite her to the supper-room (at a ball, refreshments are never handed round). Should she decline going, or has already been there, take her back to her *chaperon*, or party, and, procuring a seat for her, thank her for the pleasure the dance has afforded you.

No lady should detain her partner long in the supper-room; she may be thus forcing him to be guilty of the rudeness of breaking an engagement with another lady for the following dance.

No gentleman should linger round the supper-table. Your hostess invites you to a ball to dance, and be agreeable, not to haunt her supper-room, as if you were starving.

Avoid all absence of mind, staring, listlessness, and other eccentricities.

Never swing your arms about, and try to avoid being conspicuous in any way.

Take the partner with whom you may happen to be dancing when supper is announced to the supper-table, unless she has come with a gentleman, in which case you must not usurp his privilege. If she is disengaged, escort her to a seat in the supper-room, if possible, and see that she is served with the dishes she selects. Do not take your own supper at the same time; wait till the lady has finished; then take her back to the ball-room, and repeat the process, if necessary, with some other lonely damsel. When all the ladies have been once to the supper-room, the gentlemen may think of their own supper.

Gloves of white kid must be worn during the entire evening, and it is well to have a fresh pair in readiness to put on after supper.

On quitting a ball, it is not necessary to take a formal leave of the hostess. Indeed, it is preferable to make your departure as quietly as possible, in order to prevent the others from thinking it later than perhaps it is, and so breaking up the ball at an earlier hour than the hostess may desire.

If a gentleman escorts a lady home from a ball, she is not obliged to invite him to enter, and if she does so, he must decline the invitation. He must, however, request permission to call the following day or evening, and he must make that call.

A gentleman in a ball-room cannot be too careful not to injure the delicate frabric worn by the ladies around him. Spurs are in bad taste, even if a cavalry officer is otherwise in full uniform.

While one dance is in progress, it is not in good taste to make arrangements for another.

It is a gross breach of etiquette on the part of either a lady or a gentleman to forget a ball-room engagement.

It is not according to etiquette for married people to dance together at either a private or a public ball.

MORNING AND EVENING PARTIES.

PARTIES in the city comprise conversaziones, private concerts, private theatricals, soirées, dramatic readings, tea-parties, matinées—in fact, almost any in-door gathering together of people, exclusive of balls and dinner companies.

In the country, small dancing-parties, tea-parties, and conversaziones are also comprised under the head of parties; but the out-door occasions are of much greater number and variety: croquet parties, sailing parties, boating parties, pic-nics, private fêtes, berrying parties, nutting parties, May festivals, Fourth of July festivals—in fact, anything that will give an excuse for a day spent in out-door frolicking.

For a conversazione, under which head are included "Receptions" and "At Homes," invitations should be sent out a week beforehand. Conversation is, as the name implies, the principal occupation for the time, and where literary people are gathered together, or those engrossed in scientific matters, the sole one. For parties of young people, however, the conversazione admits of music and impromptu dances.

For all small evening parties, the host and hostess remain near the door during the early part of the evening, to receive their guests. Late comers, however, must not expect to find them still nailed to this one spot, as, after the majority of the guests are assembled, their duty is to circulate round the room and entertain them. They should, however, be quick to observe any late arrivals, and advance to welcome them as soon as possible. As the guests enter the room, the hostess should advance a step or two towards them, speaking a few words of cordial welcome, to the elder ladies first, then to the younger ones, and finally to the gentlemen. If the new comers are strangers to the rest of the guests, she must introduce them at once to those present; if, however, there are mutual friends present, it is their duty to leave the hostess after a few minutes, that she may be free to receive her other friends.

The hostess must remain constantly amongst her guests. For her to fidget in and out constantly, as if cooking the supper, or training the waiters, is a mark of low breeding. The most perfectly well-bred hostess is the one who seems to have no thought beyond the circle of her guests.

As many rooms as possible should be thrown open and supplied with objects of interest in the arts and sciences. People of some public note, whether for travel, art, learning, science, or any attainment, are often placed upon exhibition at the conversazione. If such a lion is invited, it is well to have others, even if of lesser magnitude, to prevent too much attention being concentrated upon one guest.

If a hostess sees that a *tête-à-tête* conversation is becoming dull, she must make it a trio by the introduction of some sprightly third, or change the duet by substituting another partner and carrying off one to introduce elsewhere. If, however, any conversation seems to be animated and giving pleasure, neither of the parties so engaged will thank the hostess for interruption.

If dancing is introduced, the etiquette of the ball-room is also the etiquette for the evening party. It is best for the hostess to provide a pianist, if she does not herself preside at the piano, as it is excessively ill-bred to expect part of the guests to play for the remainder to dance. Many good-natured people find themselves thus victimized—invited "because they are always so willing to play for dancing." It is a good plan in a dancing party to have ices alone handed round once or even twice during the evening, and a hot supper later, if at all. Ices, lemonade, cake, confectionery, and fruits are, however, quite sufficient refreshment for small parties.

If the evening of a party is stormy, the hostess should have a waiter at the door, with a *large* umbrella, to escort the guests from the carriages to the house, or, better still, have an awning stretched across the sidewalk.

If a party is mixed—conversation, music, and dancing, all forming a portion of the evening's entertainment—it is the part of the hostess to invite guests to sing and play, and she must be careful not to overlook any amateurs in her invitations. If a guest declines, it is in bad taste to urge the performance. If the lady of the house is herself a good performer, she must play or sing but once, and then after all others have been first invited. A guest should only be invited to play once, unless at a generally expressed desire of the remainder of the company.

It is best for amateur performers to learn a few pieces of music without depending upon their notes, as, if they send or carry notes, it is a hint that they expect to be invited to play; if they do not, they are obliged to decline when invited.

It is excessively rude to converse loudly when any one is playing or singing. If your companion does not cease talking, to listen, converse in a very low tone, and withdraw from the immediate vicinity of the performer. On the other hand, if you are invited to play, do not wait for quiet in the room, nor exhibit any annoyance if your most exquisite passages are drowned in the buzz of conversation.

A gentleman who is a good pianist may, with perfect propriety, offer his services to the hostess as orchestra for impromptu dancing, or may offer to relieve any lady so engaged, to allow her to dance. If, however, there are more ladies than gentlemen, and he is needed to fill up a set, he must not insist upon playing, but go where he is most needed.

Never offer to turn the leaves for any one playing unless you can read music rapidly; otherwise you may confuse the performer by turning too soon or too late.

Never offer to sing a second unless invited by the lady who is to sing also. The hostess may wish her friends to hear a duet, which will be disagreeable to the performers.

Members of the same family, cousins or other relatives, should not keep together in general society. They can see each other on other occasions, and the object of parties is to promote sociality, not exclusiveness.

If you are asked to play an accompaniment, do not seek to display your own talent, but play so as to afford the best support possible for the voice singing. The same rule applies to a second in any instrumental duet, which is never intended to drown the sound of the leading instrument.

When the lady of the house invites any lady guest to sing or play, the gentleman standing nearest to her should offer his arm to escort her to the piano or harp. He should stand near her during the performance of the music, and, if competent, turn the leaves of her music. She may also request him to hold her gloves, bouquet and fan. When she rises, he should conduct her to a seat, and thank her for the pleasure she has given him and others.

It is ill-bred to comment upon the piano, even if shockingly out of tune or worn out. To look at a six-octave piano and decline playing because all your music is written for seven octaves, is positively insulting to a hostess. If it is true, decline upon some other pretext.

Private concerts and theatricals ought to be very good to be successful. Professional singers should be secured for the former, and if amateurs sing, they must be very confident of their own powers before making the attempt to appear before an audience, even of personal friends. Between the parts, conversation may flow, but is rude in the extreme during the performances. The best hours are from two to six or from eight to eleven P.M. The rooms should be arranged so as to allow a clear space at one end for the performers; the guests should be seated, and a general silence prevail excepting during the intervals of the performance. If the concert is divided into two parts, it is quite permissible to rise during the intermission, promenade if agreeable, meet friends, and change seats, being careful to be seated again when the performance re-commences.

For private theatricals, only the best amateurs should be retained. It is very rude to talk during the acts, and while applause should not be too boisterous, disapproval by hissing or otherwise is a thing unheard of. Ices and light refreshments should be handed round between the acts. Where there is no arrangement for a private theatre, and where the curtain is hung, as is most common, between the folding-doors, the audience-room must be filled with chairs or benches in rows, and, if possible, the back rows raised higher than the others. These are often removed at the close of the performance, and the guests then converse or dance.

To beat time or hum the air at a concert is in extremely bad taste.

It is the part of the hostess at a private concert and private theatricals—which latter include charades, tableaux, proverbs, and dramatic readings—to arrange the programmes and apportion the parts, unless she appoints a stage-manager amongst her guests. The performers should seek to aid her by perfect good-nature in accepting her arrangements, and by willingness to accept any allotted part, even if distasteful or obscure. All cannot be first, and the performer who good-naturedly accepts a small part, and performs it *well*, will probably be invited to a more conspicuous position on the next occasion. The hostess or host must never take conspicuous parts, unless they are solicited to do so by all the rest of the *corps dramatique.*

Nothing but the most absolute necessity, or an excuse from some very grave cause, should prevent the attendance of any one who has undertaken a part. It is a positive insult to the rest of the party to inconvenience them by remaining away upon some trivial excuse, for the smallest part must be filled by somebody, and it is not easy to furnish substitutes upon such occasions.

The hostess should consult each performer before allotting to them a part, and endeavor to suit each one.

Private concerts and private theatricals should be followed by a supper, as they are fatiguing for the performers, and oftentimes as much so to the audience.

If a party are invited to an informal dramatic reading, it is not necessary to divide the room, excepting by a large table, upon which the books are placed. The host or hostess, while endeavoring to give to each guest the most favorable opportunity to display their own powers, should still, if they are good readers, be ready to oblige their guests by reading also, carefully avoiding any attempt to outshine them.

Matinées are usually held in the open air, in some good ground, in which a brass band should be playing, and plenty of good flowers displayed, embellished by the best dressed people it is possible to assemble together. There are not any introductions; people amuse themselves as best they can. Luncheon may be spread in-doors, or upon tables under the trees, or if tents are erected, inside of these. Fruits, ices, salads, cold meats, confectionery—in short, any cold collation, with wine, tea, and coffee, should be served. Full morning dress is most appropriate.

Croquet parties are very fashionable, and meet generally at about three P.M. The host should be careful to have his grounds well shaded, his mallets, balls, and other arrangements in perfect order. Seats for such guests as are not playing should be scattered about in shady places. Refreshments may be handed round between the games, or arranged as for matinées.

Within the past few years, a species of entertainment of a past generation has been revived in England, and some attempts have been made to introduce it in this country. It was, and is, called the "Kettledrum." Tea and coffee, with biscuit and cake, are served round from five to half-past five. Any one in the visiting circle of the house may go without an invitation; the dress is full morning dress, and the guests dance until seven o'clock. From them guests often go to dinner parties, and thence to balls, so that a man may be considered to be in harness to society from five P.M. to 4 A.M., and to be rather hardly driven, too.

Ceremony is laid aside upon these occasions, and people act with greater freedom than at more formal gatherings.

In country parties, ceremony is often required, even upon occasions where more freedom of action would be desirable. Inattention to this matter may give offence, as the hostess may fancy herself slighted merely because she is not city-bred.

Avoid in country parties treading upon delicate ground, talking of local squabbles, church matters, or the acknowledged feud of the village.

Be punctual to the time stated for any kind of a country party, as one late arrival may delay the carriages, boats, or other conveyances of an entire party. Many of these expeditions start at a very early hour, to avoid the road during the heat of the day, and if you accept the invitation, you must relinquish your morning nap and appear at the appointed time. Seek out the hostess upon your arrival, and if you can in any way assist her, either by running for tardy servants, packing luncheon hampers, arranging the order of vehicles, or any other *last* duties, do so with alacrity.

Private fêtes in the country correspond to matinées in town, and the same rules apply.

At pic-nics, whether water or land parties, etiquette is set at naught; yet the true gentleman and lady will never leave true courtesy and politeness at home, even if they lay aside forms and ceremonies. Everybody is to enjoy the time and freedom as much as possible, "within the limits of becoming mirth;" yet an act of rudeness, a disregard of the gentle and delicate attentions of society, will never increase the pleasure.

Gentlemen at pic-nics must consent to become waiters, guides, servants to the ladies; must "scale mountains," climb trees, perform any feats desired by the fair tyrants, if they fancy "that lovely flower," or "exquisite bunch of sea-weed," in impossible-to-get-at places. If on a fishing party, it is the gentlemen's place to bait the hooks for the fair anglers, to assist them in landing their prey, to find them shady nooks for seats, and in every way to assist them. If nutting or berrying are the objects of the party, the gentlemen must climb the nut-trees, seek out the berry-bushes, carry double allowances of baskets and kettles, and be ready for any assistance required in climbing fences or scrambling over rocks. By the way, the etiquette for climbing a fence is for the gentleman to go over as gracefully as possible, turn his back upon the lady, and not look round until she claims his hand to spring from the topmost bar. She will not thank him if he insists upon shoving her over first, or watches her while she climbs up.

Boisterous deportment is not in good taste. Even the most romping games may be conducted as becomes ladies and gentlemen, not as clowns. Couples should avoid straying too long or too far from their companions.

Even if the luncheon or dinner is spread on the grass, or eaten out of a basket, gentlemen will see to the comfort of the ladies before eating themselves, and, need I say, the freedom from the restraints of the table affords no excuse for gluttony or rudeness of any description.

On returning from a pic-nic, the thanks of the party are due to the originators of it, and should be paid by each one before the company disperses.

Singing a comic song is a dangerous experiment, as you may be personal without intending it. An English lady of rank, speaking of an evening party, says: "At an evening party, given expressly in honor of a distinguished lady of color, we heard a thoughtless amateur dash into the broadly comic, but terribly appropriate 'nigger' song of 'Sally, Come Up.' Before he had got through the first verse, he had perceived his mistake, and was so overwhelmed with shame that he could scarcely preserve sufficient presence of mind to carry him through to the end."

A modern writer of talent says: "Your pleasure at any party will depend far more upon what you take with you into the room than upon what you find there. Ambition, vanity, pride, will all go with anxiety, and you will probably carry them all home again, with the additional burden of disappointment. Even if they are all gratified, you will know that others are disliking you, even if envious of you. To go with a sincere desire to please others by amiability, good-nature and sympathy will probably result in your own popularity, and if you entirely forget yourself, you will be astonished to find how much others insist upon remembering you."

If at any morning or evening party you meet a distinguished guest, it is ill-bred to follow him from one place to another, listening to every word he utters, and making him have the uncomfortable sensation of being "stared at."

Impromptu charades are a very popular amusement at the present day, at both in-door and out-door parties. If you have no talent for them, you will only confuse others and make yourself appear absurd by insisting upon taking a part; but even if you are dull, do not refuse your assistance if it is really required, trying, by tact and modesty, to cover up any deficiency in wit or talent.

The best rule for the management of parties, be they in-door or out-door, morning or evening, city or country, is to endeavor to find out the wishes of the majority of the guests and act upon that knowledge. To force a large party of people to listen to awkward, bungling charades, because two or three amateur actors desire to "show off," proves a want of tact in the hostess; to allow a few young people to guide the entertainments in a large assembly of older and graver ones, is in equally bad taste; it is, of course, better to assemble together as far as possible only those who are likely to be congenial and interested in the same subjects; but this is not always possible, and where the company is mixed, the republican spirit should preside, and the "majority rule."

One word of warning to all who give parties. You can never tell what ruin may be commencing when you urge wines or intoxicating beverages upon your young guests. You may be the first to stimulate the appetite; you may renew a passion that has been subdued; you may turn a wavering will from the hardly gained resolution to abstain. There are instances, not a few, but many, where the love of liquor, conquered and subdued, has been revived in fiercest heat by cordials, brandied peaches, wine-sauces, and similar apparently innocent refreshments. It is better to appear mean than to tempt to ruin, and in these days of temperance movements, no lady will be censured or misunderstood who banishes every drop of intoxicating liquor from her table.

VISITING.

Never pay any visit upon a general invitation. The Spanish hidalgo, who declares to you that his house, lands, all that he has, are yours, would be greatly surprised if you appropriated any of his things. It is the same thing, more or less, with people elsewhere who give people general invitations to take up their quarters in their houses.

There are instances of visits of a month's duration being made upon the invitation, "If you visit B——, I hope that you will not forget that I reside there, and will be very happy to see you." Yet, even where friends are not newly made, but of long standing, it is best not to pay visits unless by special invitation. A thousand events may occur to render it inconvenient for one friend to have company that cannot be known to another, hundreds of miles, perhaps, away. If a friend really desires to extend hospitality to another, she will send her an invitation, which can be accepted with the prospect of mutual convenience and pleasure.

Even in travelling, if you are unexpectedly detained in a city where you have friends, do not drive to their house uninvited. Go first to a hotel, and let them know of your arrival, leaving it optional with them to extend hospitality. To drive at once to the house, with your baggage, forces an invitation, which may cause much annoyance and inconvenience, even if they are really glad to see you, and it also renders you liable to be accused of meanness and a desire to save your hotel bill. If you are afraid your friends will feel hurt if you do not "make their house your home," at least write to them and ascertain if they can conveniently receive you as you pass through their city. Even with relatives, it is better to announce your coming, that your hostess may so arrange her engagements and household as to leave her time to really enjoy your visit.

A special invitation should specify who is invited, and no one not mentioned should go. "Love me, love my dog," is a proverb that will not apply in such cases. A person who is invited to visit at a friend's house is not at liberty to bring children and servants who were not included in the invitation. A wife may, of course, accompany her husband, unless there be special reason to the contrary, and a husband must always have the opportunity of accompanying his wife, or joining her.

If the length of your visit is not specified in your invitation, a week is a good limit for your stay. At all events, make a move at the end of that time, and if you are invited to stay longer, and know that it is convenient for you to do so, the time can then be definitely decided upon.

When you receive an invitation by letter, answer it at the earliest possible moment, and say decidedly whether you accept or decline it. To leave your friends in doubt may prevent the same invitation being extended to others. As soon as possible after accepting an invitation, write and let your friends know by what train to expect you, and keep your engagement, that you may not keep any one waiting for you at the station for nothing. If you are unavoidably detained, write or telegraph and say so, naming another hour for your arrival.

In inviting a friend to pay you a visit, name a season when will you will be able to devote most of your time to their entertainment. Have always a room devoted especially to your guest, and be sure that no one intrudes there without a special invitation, and never enter it yourself without an invitation to do so. Before the arrival of a guest, see yourself that the room is in perfect order, well warmed if in winter, shaded and cool if in summer; let there be every convenience for bath and change of dress, and writing materials and stamps ready to write if desired before unpacking. Have always a feather bed and mattress, both feather and hair pillows upon the bed, that your guest may have the choice. Many prefer feathers in the warmest weather, others a mattress even in winter. Let the fire, in winter, be made every morning before your guest rises, and keep a good supply of fuel in the room.

It is the duty of the host to send a carriage to the depôt to meet an expected visitor, and if possible to go himself. After a warm welcome, show the guest at once to the room prepared, and give ample time for a bath and change of dress, if it is in the day time. If the arrival is late in the evening, have a substantial supper prepared, and then allow the traveller to retire, being careful that on the first arrival the breakfast can be ready at a late hour, that your friend may not be disturbed to breakfast with the family.

It is the duty of the hostess to share the meals of a guest, no matter how irregular; but any truly polite person will pay strict attention to the customary meal times.

When staying with friends, endeavor as much as possible to conform to their regular habits. Be punctual at meal times. Ascertain over-night the hour for breakfast, and be particular to be dressed in time for it. After breakfast, it is customary to leave visitors to their own devices, unless some special arrangement is made for the forenoon; but the hostess should introduce her guests to the piano, billiard-table, portfolios library—any device for passing time at her command; and the visitor should accept this hint, and expect no further attention during the forenoon.

It is, however, the duty of the host and hostess to accompany their guests to any points of interest in their city or neighborhood, to accompany them if they desire to do any shopping, and if they have any special habit, as rising late, napping in the afternoon, or other little self-indulgence, to see that they are never disturbed in it.

It is also a kindly courtesy, if your friends have acquaintances in the city beside yourself, to inform them of their arrival, even if strangers to yourself, and invite them to call, dine, or take tea during the visit. If you give your guests a party, you must invite all their friends in the city, even if they are strangers to yourself. Invite them in your guest's name, enclosing your own invitation in theirs.

Host and hostess should give up as much of their time as possible to their guests, and should see that they are amused and taken care of. It is a mistake, however, to suppose that visitors require constant attention, and they should be careful not to "bore" them by over-attention, which savors of fussiness. A guest will often under such circumstances long for a lonely hour to devote to music, reading, or sewing, but does not like to express the desire.

The truest courtesy is for the host to make his visitor feel as much at home as possible, and for the visitor to disturb the host's household as little as possible.

Where a lady is visiting, she may with perfect propriety offer to assist her hostess in her household duties or family sewing; but if she declines, it is bad taste to insist. She should, however, leave her hostess free for such duties in the morning, being always ready to join her in the sitting-room when she is at leisure.

It is a graceful way to acknowledge the kindness of your hostess to work whilst with her upon some piece of embroidery, a piano-cover, a sofa-cushion, or some article of dress, which you present to her when finished as a memento of your visit.

For a guest to make outside engagements, disregard the meal times, visit without consulting the host or hostess, is to treat the house of a friend as if it were a hotel, and is not only rude, but positively insulting.

It is best, if you are visiting a large city, and desire to do shopping or to transact business, to select the hours when you know your entertainers are otherwise engaged for such business, and not tax them to accompany you, unless they have similar affairs requiring attention, when it may be pleasanter to have company.

Neither hostess nor guest may accept any invitations which do not include the other.

If either hostess or visitor is in mourning, the other must decline all invitations during the visit, giving that as a reason. It is always accepted in society as sufficient excuse.

If any sudden trouble comes into a house where you are visiting, try to be of service. Let your friend feel that you have not visited her for gayety alone, but are glad to sympathize in her trouble. If sickness or death come, share the nursing, try to relieve the hostess of some of her family cares, if it is only taking the children into your own room or out for a walk; be ready to do the shopping required for mourning, and take away every painful detail you can. There is no comfort so great as a really useful sympathizing friend in times of trouble; yet if relatives come and require rooms, if you find you are a restraint and can be of no use, it is the truest kindness to shorten your visit, and leave the mourners free to comfort each other.

When visiting, never depend upon your host for writing or sewing materials; but it is a delicate attention for you, if hostess, to have your guest's room amply supplied with both.

It is extremely rude for visitors to make comparisons between the house at which they are visiting and others where they have enjoyed hospitality. To inform your hostess indirectly that her house, furniture, table, or servants are inferior to those of other friends, is insulting, and it is as much so to cast the slur upon the first house visited by vaunting the superiority of the second.

To a certain extent, use your friend's servants as your own—wholly so as far as your own personal wants require their services. Ask for whatever you want in your own room, and give any requisite directions to the servant who waits upon you. Do not trouble the mistress of the house with matters which in your own house you would give to a servant. At the same time, avoid being troublesome; put out your own washing, and any extra work you require done, and never call upon the servants at hours when they are otherwise employed.

If you are unfortunate enough during a visit to injure any article of furniture in your own room, have it repaired or replaced at once at your own expense.

It is a graceful compliment for a gentleman during a visit to bring flowers, fruit, books, or confectionery occasionally to the hostess, and a lady friend will be gratefully remembered if she is kind to the children.

If a gift is made, it must be to the hostess, or if there are several children, to the youngest. If children are over twelve years old, it is better to give any present to the mother; but you will never give offence by a gift to the baby. A gentleman may give silver or baby jewelry, and a lady a piece of handsome needlework. You may be sure the parents will find no fault with this acknowledgment of their hospitality.

Always hold yourself at the disposal of those in whose house you are staying. If they propose to ride, drive, walk, or otherwise occupy the day, you must take it for granted that these plans are made with reference to your enjoyment. You should receive them with cheerfulness and enter into them with alacrity, doing your best to seem pleased, and be pleased, by the efforts made to entertain you. Never mind if it is the twentieth time you have driven to "see the lovely view from the hill four miles from here," or you have paid a dozen previous visits to "that beautiful waterfull just above the lake;" you must find a new tree to admire, or a new point to sketch every time you go.

It is not expected that the host or hostess can devote the entire day to guests. Sir Walter Scott's conduct towards his guests at Abbotsford furnishes a model of hospitality. He never saw them till dinner; but whilst he was busily engaged in writing, he left his house, servants, carriages, horses, and grounds at their entire disposal.

Byron gives a perfect picture of guest life at a country house:

"The gentlemen got up betimes to shoot,
Or hunt; the young, because they liked the sport—
The first thing boys like, after play and fruit;
The middle-aged, to make the day more short;
For *ennui* is a growth of English root,
Though nameless in our language—we retort
The fact for words, and let the French translate
That awful yawn which sleep cannot abate.

"The elderly walked through the library,
And tumbled books, or criticized the pictures,
Or sauntered through the garden piteously,
And made upon the hot-house several strictures;
Or rode a nag which trotted not too high,
Or in the morning papers read their lectures;
Or on the watch their longing eyes would fix,
Longing at sixty for the hour of six.

"But none were 'gené;' the great hour of union
Was rung by dinner's knell! till then all were
Masters of their own time—or in communion,
Or solitary, as they chose to bear
The hours, which how to pass to few is known.
Each rose up at his own, and had to spare
What time he chose for dress, and broke his fast
When, where, and how he chose for that repast."

In this country, hospitality is but seldom conducted on the lavish broad scale possible at an English country residence; but, as far as possible, it is better to allow guests perfect liberty for breakfast hour and morning employments.

Great discretion must be used among guests to avoid all criticism on their host, his friends, his household, his manner of living, and all that coucerns him. If anything goes wrong during the visit, one should seem not to see it. If the dinner is late, it is very impolite to appear impatient. If any plan falls to the ground, no comments or disapproval must be indulged in, and no disappointment betrayed. If the children of the house are fractious, or noisy, or ill-bred, a visitor must never find fault with their behavior.

The same caution must be exercised in the treatment of your friend's friends. They may be such as you do not care to become intimate with; but you must not evince dislike or special avoidance, and must always have recourse rather to a negative than a positive line of conduct. A person of tact can always keep people at a distance without hurting their feelings.

Your host's horses, carriages, books, and grounds should be even more carefully used than if they were your own. A good-natured man will delight in seeing his visitors enjoy all the good things he places at their disposal; but they should not abuse his indulgence. To ride a horse too far or too fast, to dog's-ear or blot the books in the library, to gather choice and favorite flowers, are all signs of an under-bred and selfish nature. Above all, we should be thoughtful in our treatment of the servants, never commenting upon their shortcomings, or scolding them.

The religious opinions, especially of those from whom we are receiving hospitality, must on no account be shocked, scoffed at, or in any way treated with a want of respect. If our friends go regularly to church, we should accompany them there; or, without remark, repair to the place of worship most agreeable to our own religious convictions. If family prayers are read, we should endeavor to be present. If silent grace is the custom at meal times, our heads must also bow, and a short mental prayer be said. If the Sunday is observed with great strictness, we should refrain from any pursuits to which objection could possibly be made, even if they appear to ourselves perfectly proper and innocent. In short, we must remember that for the time the feelings and prejudices of the host and hostess are our own.

There is no occasion when it is more necessary to remember that social intercourse is made up of innumerable little acts of kindness, self-denial, charity, chivalry, and good-fellowship, than when a number of people find themselves thrown together for companionship in the house of some mutual friend.

Letters delivered in the presence of the host or hostess, or when the other guests are present, must not be opened until the receiver asks permission to read them.

A lady may never offer to pay any of the expenses incurred by taking her about—carriage hire, steamboat fares, or such outlay—nor must a gentleman do so unless he is the only gentleman of the party. It will then be well for the hostess, before starting, to hand him the necessary tickets previously purchased.

When a guest is ready to leave you, be sure that the trunks are strapped and ticketed, a carriage ready in good season, a luncheon prepared for refreshment upon the journey, a substantial meal ready in good season for comfortable enjoyment of it, and the departure made as pleasant as possible.

"Welcome the coming, speed the parting guest." It is the first duty of the guest, after returning home, to write to the host or hostess, expressing the pleasure derived from the visit, and mentioning each member of the family by name, desiring to be remembered to all.

STREET ETIQUETTE.

When a gentleman recognizes a friend in the course of his walk, he must lift his hat with the hand farthest from him. Lifting the hat is a sufficient recognition between gentlemen; but in meeting a lady, an old gentleman, or a clergyman, it is necessary to bow also.

If a gentleman wishes to shake hands with a friend, he must lift his hat with the left hand, leaving the right free to extend. Never must he give his left hand, or extend a portion of the right. The whole right hand is *en règle.*

A lady must recognize a gentleman, by bowing, before he is at liberty to acknowledge an acquaintance with her. Should she bow, he must lift his hat and bow also. If he is sufficiently barbarous to have a cigar in his mouth, he must remove it while bowing to a lady.

If a gentleman is walking with a lady, he should insist upon carrying any book, parcel, or umbrella she may have with her.

No gentleman may smoke when walking with a lady. He should even decline to do so though he may be asked to continue smoking.

Should a lady stop a gentleman to speak, she must make a slight inclination of the head as a token of dismissal, and he must accept it as such, bow, and leave her.

No lady will be guilty of the vulgarity of sucking the head of her parasol in the street.

To eat anything, even confectionery, in the street, is a sign of low breeding.

A gentleman must give a lady, an old gentleman, or clergyman with whom he may be walking, the upper side (nearest the houses) of the pavement.

If a gentleman meets a lady friend who is walking with any one he does not know, he must not stop, nor must he stop if his companion is unacquainted with a lady friend whom he may chance to meet. The lady, however, has a perfect right to do as she likes. If she should stop, the strangers must be introduced, and none of the group should go on and wait, whether the introduction be agreeable or not.

A lady should avoid walking very rapidly. It is very ungraceful and unbecoming.

Swinging the arms is an awkward and ill-bred habit.

For a lady to run across the street, to avoid a carriage passing, is not only ill-bred, but exceedingly dangerous.

To attempt to cross the street between the carriages of a funeral procession is rude and disrespectful; and we cannot but commend the foreign custom of removing the hat, and standing in a respectful attitude until the melancholy train has passed.

When a gentleman is walking alone, he must always turn aside to give the upper side of the pavement to a lady, to any one carrying a heavy load, to a clergyman, or to an old gentleman.

Never push violently through a crowd. If a gentleman or lady is really in haste, a few courteous words will open a passage more quickly than the most vigorous pushing or shoving.

If a lady is caught in a shower, and a gentleman offers an umbrella, she may accept it, if he is going in the same direction as herself and accompanies her. If not, and he still insists, etiquette requires the return of the umbrella as soon as the lady reaches her destination. No lady may accept this courtesy from a strange gentleman, but must decline it firmly, but politely.

Stopping to stare in the shop-windows is against the rules of strict etiquette.

If a gentleman and lady are obliged to cross a narrow walk, plank, or slippery place, the lady may go first, and the gentleman walk close behind her, to aid her if needful. If the place is short, then the gentleman should go first, and then offer his hand to assist the lady across. If a gentleman meet a lady or old gentleman at such a crossing, he may, with perfect propriety, assist them in crossing, even if perfect strangers to him.

A gentleman must hold his hat in his hand if he stops to inquire his own way, or to direct another.

If a gentleman sees a lady alone hesitating at a bad crossing, or leaving a carriage at an awkward place, he may offer his hand to assist her in crossing or alighting, raise his hat, bow, and pass on. A lady may, with perfect propriety, accept such assistance from a stranger, thanking him, and returning his bow.

If a lady leaves an omnibus or car alone, the gentleman nearest the door should alight, assist her out, and enter the omnibus again.

Gentlemen should always pass up the fare of ladies in an omnibus.

A lady is not expected to recognize any acquaintance on the opposite side of the street.

In a public conveyance, a gentleman should offer his seat to any lady who is standing, and the lady should thank him audibly for the courtesy. To turn his back upon her at once, and thus force her to accept the courtesy in silence or shout her thanks, is rude. A polite bow exchanged is a sufficient acknowledgment.

Loud talking and laughing in the street are sure signs of vulgarity.

Never look back after any one passing; it is extremely ill-bred.

Staring is a mark of low breeding.

Whispering in a public conveyance is excessively rude.

Never call out loudly to an acquaintance who may be passing.

"Cutting" is to be avoided, if possible. There are other ways of convincing a man that you will not know him; yet, to young ladies, it is sometimes the only means available to rid them of a troublesome acquaintance. Cutting consists in publicly ignoring, by deed, and, if need be, by word, the acquaintance of the offensive person. A stiff bow will usually effect the desired object; if not, a purposed non-recognition will probably succeed. It must be a very bad case where it is necessary to tell one you "have not the pleasure of an acquaintance" with them. A gentleman must never, under any circumstances, cut a lady; an unmarried lady may not cut a married one, nor a young man an old one.

George IV., when Prince of Wales, once cut Beau Brummell, with whom he had quarrelled. The pair met in St. James-street, each walking with a companion; the companions stopped to speak, but the Prince did not see Brummell. The latter, to be revenged, and knowing the horror the Prince had of being considered corpulent, said to his companion, in a stage whisper, before the others were out of ear-shot, "Who is your fat friend?"

On meeting and passing people in the street, keep to your right hand, except when giving the upper side of the pavement as before mentioned.

Let a lady walking with a gentleman have always the upper side of the pavement, even if he changes sides at every turning.

Young persons, meeting elderly friends in the street, should wait for a recognition before speaking, and then bow respectfully. To nod carelessly at an old person is rude, if not actually insulting.

If you meet two gentlemen in the street, and wish to speak to one of them, apologize to the other, and make the detention as brief as possible.

If a gentleman is about to enter or to leave a store, and meets a lady in the door-way, he must stand aside, raise his hat, and wait for her to pass. If the door is closed, and she is going the same way as himself, he must pass before her, bow, saying, "Permit me," or "allow me to open the door," open it, and hold it open until she has passed.

A gentleman walking with a lady should endeavor to accommodate his steps to hers, not force her to stride along or trot with short steps or his long ones.

Etiquette is too often disregarded in that grand aim of most ladies' excursions on the street—shopping. True politeness will lead a lady to pay some attention to the feelings of the clerks and women in attendance, and they are quick to observe who are lady-like, and who are not, in their intercourse with them.

Do not enter a store unless you have some errand.

Ask for what you want as explicitly as possible, and do not take the time of the attendants by examining fifty things that you do not want.

If you do not intend to purchase goods, but wish to examine them for future selections, say so.

Never try to cheapen goods. If the price is too high for the quality offered, or will not suit your purse, look elsewhere for what will better suit you.

Do not stand hesitating at a counter. Make up your mind quickly, or leave the store to make your decision, even if you return again.

Be careful not to injure goods by handling.

Never ask for patterns without apologizing for the trouble, and not then unless you really intend to return for the goods, as when you are shopping for a friend, or wish for the judgment or taste of another person.

Never give unnecessary trouble.

It is best to have all bundles sent home; they are awkward additions to a walking-dress, and boys are kept for that purpose in all well-arranged stores.

Never keep a clerk waiting while you chat with a friend. If you desire to speak with your acquaintances, stand aside, that the clerk may understand he is released for the time, and free to wait upon other customers.

Never call away a clerk who is waiting upon some one else. Wait, if you have business with an especial clerk, until you see that he is disengaged.

Sneering remarks upon goods is rude in the extreme. If they do not suit you, you are not obliged to buy them; but spare your comments.

Lounging over a counter is ill-bred.

Putting your elbows on a counter is rude.

Pushing aside another person is an act of ill-breeding.

You must never take hold of a piece of goods another person is examining. Wait until it is replaced upon the counter, when you are at liberty to take it up.

Stage asides or whispering in a store are rude.

It is rude to interrupt friends you may meet in a store, to ask their attention to your purchases, before they have finished making their own. It is as rude to offer your opinion, unasked, upon their judgment or taste in selection of goods.

A gentleman walking with two ladies may offer an arm to each of them, and they may thus sandwich him if they wish; but under no circumstances may a lady take the arms of gentlemen at each side of her.

If a gentleman is walking with two ladies in a rain-storm, and there is but one umbrella, he should give it to his companions and walk outside. Nothing can be more absurd than to see a gentleman walking between two ladies holding an umbrella, which perfectly protects himself, and sends little streams of water from every point on the dresses of the ladies he is supposed to be sheltering.

It is in bad taste to talk of personal matters in the street, or to call loudly the names of persons you may mention. It is impossible to say who may be near to you. To discuss friends by name in a public conveyance of any kind is rude in the extreme.

If you meet a friend with whom you wish to shake hands, never put out your own until you are quite near, as nothing looks more awkward than hands extended to grasp each other two or three yards apart.

Never turn a corner at full speed, or you may find yourself knocked down or knocking down another by the violent contact.

Never bow from a store to a person on the street, or from the street to a person in a store.

Never talk politics or religion in a public conveyance.

Never stop to quarrel with a hack-driver. Pay his fare, and dismiss him; if you have any complaint to make, take his number, and make it to the proper authorities. To keep a lady standing while you are disputing with a hack-man is extremely rude.

It is a sign of ill-breeding to change your seat in a car or omnibus. If you are unfortunate enough to have a neighbor who is positively annoying and unendurable, it is better to get out and take the next conveyance than to move to the other side. A gentleman may move from a crowded side to one left comparatively vacant; but a lady should not do this.

In a city, or in any lonely place, a lady must avoid being alone after nightfall, if possible. It exposes her, not only to insult, but often to positive danger. It is very much the custom in small country places for two ladies to take evening walks; but it is better to have the protection of a gentleman if convenient.

It is better for a lady to decline entering a car or an omnibus that is already full. She must either stand up or force some polite gentleman to do so. It is better to wait for the next conveyance.

RIDING AND DRIVING.

The rule of the road, both in riding and driving, is always to—"Keep to the right, as the law directs."

In inviting a lady to ride, if a gentleman cannot offer the use of his own horses, or the lady does not name a horse to which she has been accustomed, he must be careful to select one of proved gentleness, and trained to the side-saddle and riding-skirt. It is exceedingly dangerous to allow a lady to mount a horse which may be entirely strange to a lady's hand or habit; and it is not well to trust this important matter to a livery-stable keeper or servant.

A gentleman must be punctual to the appointed time, as it is disagreeable for a lady to sit waiting in-doors in a riding-habit. The lady, too, must exercise strict punctuality, that the horses may not become restive from long standing.

Arrived at the house of his fair companion, the gentleman must carefully examine the entire furniture of her horse. He must test the firmness of the saddle and girths, examine well the stirrup-leather, guard against the danger of any buckle allowing a tongue of leather to slip, see that the curb, bridle, headstall, and reins are in perfect order; for the entire control of the horse is lost if one of these breaks or slips. Leaving these matters to the stable-men entirely, is unsafe, as the constant handling of the harness is apt to make them careless in fastening and testing it.

It is the duty of the gentleman to see the lady comfortably seated in the saddle before he mounts himself. Having first asked permission, he leads her to the horse. A groom should not be allowed to render any assistance, if a gentleman is present, excepting to hold the horse's head. The lady stands, with her skirt gathered in her left hand, on the near side of the horse, her right hand on the pommel of the saddle, and her face turned towards the horse's head. The gentleman should stand at the horse's shoulder, facing the lady, and stoop so that her left foot may rest in his hand. When the lady makes a spring, the gentleman should, with gentle firmness, steadily and promptly help her foot up; and when she is in the saddle, he should put her foot in the stirrup, and smooth her skirt. It requires some practice to properly assist a lady into the saddle. If the hand is not perfectly steady, it is very unpleasant, and any jerking motion is not only disagreeable, but positively dangerous.

After the lady is in the saddle, her escort should stand beside her until she has arranged her skirt, got a firm foothold in the stirrup, and has her reins and whip in order. He may then mount his own horse, and take his position on the lady's right.

In riding with two ladies, if both are good horsewomen, the gentleman should ride to the right of both; but if they are inexperienced, it is better for him to ride between them, to be ready to assist them if necessary.

A lady must always give the pace.

A gentleman must never touch a lady's horse unless she actually requires his aid; but he should be very watchful and ready for the most prompt attention if it is needed.

If a gentleman on horseback meet a lady who is walking, and stops to speak to her, he must dismount until she bows and leaves him.

A gentleman must go forward whenever a gate is to be opened or an obstruction to be removed, and clear the way for the lady; he must leap first when there is a fence or ditch to be crossed; he must pay all tolls; must first test any dangerous-looking place, and must try to select the most desirable roads.

In dismounting, a gentleman must offer a lady his right hand, taking her left, and using his own left as a step for her foot, declining it gently as soon as she rises from the saddle, and before she springs. To spring from the saddle is not only awkward, but dangerous, and will often confuse a gentleman who is accustomed only to the proper mode of assisting the ladies to whom he offers his services as escort.

No gentlemen will force a lady to ride faster than she may find agreeable, by an endeavor to display his own horsemanship.

A gentleman must be careful to protect his lady companion from the dust and mud, as far as possible; and if there is a choice of side for shade, he may, with propriety, ride upon her left, or fall a little behind her, to allow her to take advantage of it.

In riding with an elderly gentlemen, a younger man should extend all the courtesies of the road, the shady side, the choice of speed, the choice also of direction, and, if there be a difference, the best horse.

In a carriage, where a coachman is outside, the seat on the right hand, facing the horses, is the seat of honor, and should be given to a lady, an elderly gentleman, or the guest.

In entering a carriage, be careful that your back is towards the seat you wish to occupy.

The seat facing the horses is always left by gentleman for ladies. If a lady and gentleman alone enter a carriage together, the gentleman must take the seat opposite to the lady, unless she invites him to sit beside her.

A gentleman be should careful, in entering a carriage, not to trample upon ladies' dresses, shut their shawls in the door, or commit any other gaucheries. It is quite an art to enter or leave a carriage gracefully.

In quitting a carriage, a gentleman must go first, even though he may have to trouble the ladies by stepping across the carriage, and he should then help the ladies to alight, taking care not to allow the wheel to soil their dresses. If there be a man-servant with the carriage, a gentleman will allow him to lower the steps, and hold the door open; but he must on no account allow him to help the ladies out while he himself stands by.

A gentleman will always convey the orders of the ladies to the coachman.

If the carriage is driven by the gentleman himself, there are many little points of etiquette which demand attention.

When a gentleman is about to take a lady, an older gentleman, or a guest to drive, he must drive as close as possible to the mounting block or curb, head his horse towards the middle of the road, and back his buggy or wagon slightly, separating the fore and hind wheels as much as possible. This is especially necessary when a lady is to ascend to the wagon, as it gives space for her dress to avoid the contact of the wheels, and allows room for the driver to tuck her dress in after she is seated. It is best to have always a carriage-blanket to cover entirely the skirt of a lady's dress, that the mud of the road may not splash it.

When there is a post, it is always safest to hitch the horse securely, and give both hands to the lady's service. Never allow the horse to stand without some hold upon him; if there is no post, the reins must be held firmly in one hand, while the other assists the lady.

No gentleman will *show off* his driving, if he finds his companion timid. He will adopt the pace most agreeable to her, even if it condemns him to a funeral slowness.

It is courtesy for the owner of a wagon, when driving a gentleman friend, to offer him the reins, but the offer should never be accepted. If, when driving a long distance, with a hard-mouthed horse, the companion can really relieve a tired driver, it is then both courteous and kind to offer to take the reins for a time; but it is not etiquette so to offer under any other circumstances.

If you offer a seat in a private carriage to any friends you may meet whilst abroad, you must accompany them to their destination, no matter how far it may be out of your own way.

For a gentleman, when driving with a lady, to put his arm across the back of the seat, around her, is a piece of impertinence which any well-bred lady will very justly resent.

If offered a seat in the carriage of a gentleman friend, you should motion him to be seated first; but if he stands aside for you, bow, and precede him.

After assisting a lady to her seat, be certain that her parasol, shawl, and fan are all conveniently placed for her use before you take your own seat. Allow her all the space you can, and be especially careful that the motion of your arms does not incommode her.

If a lady wishes to leave a carriage, and the gentleman remains in it to wait her return, he must alight to assist her out, and also when she enters it again, even if he resumes his seat during her absence.

It is a graceful act to leave a carriage in the proper manner. In England, young ladies are instructed in the manner of entering and leaving a carriage. M. Mercy D'Argenteau, an ambassador of the last century, tells an anecdote illustrative of the importance of this. He says: "The Princess of Hesse-Darmstadt having been desired by the Empress of Austria to bring her three daughters to court, in order that her Imperial Majesty might choose one of them for a wife to one of her sons, drove up in her coach to the palace gate.

"Scarcely had they entered the presence, when, before even speaking to them, the Empress went up to the second daughter, and, taking her by the hand, said: 'I choose this young lady.'

"The mother, astonished at the suddenness of her choice, inquired what had actuated her.

"'I watched the young ladies get out of their carriage,' said the Empress. 'Your eldest daughter stepped on her dress, and only saved herself from falling by an awkward scramble; the youngest jumped from the coach to the ground, without touching the steps; the second, just lifting her dress in front, so as she descended to show the point of her shoe, calmly stepped from the carriage to the ground, neither hurriedly nor stiffly, but with grace and dignity. She is fit to be an empress. Her eldest sister is too awkward; her youngest, too wild.'"

Riding and driving are accomplishments in which it is very desirable for all ladies and gentlemen to be proficient. To ride well, one must be taught early, and have practice. Like swimming, riding cannot be learned from theoretical teaching.

Lord Herbert, of Cherbury, says: 'A good rider, on a good horse, is as much above himself and others as the world can make him."

TRAVELLING.

THERE are many little points of etiquette and courteous observances which, if attended to, serve very materially to lighten the tedium and fatigue of travel, the non-observance of them being attended with proportionally disagreeable effects. No situation can be named where the difference between the well-bred and ill-bred of either sex is more marked than when they are upon a journey; and in this country, where all classes are thrown into contact in the various public conveyances, the annoyance of rude company can scarcely be exaggerated.

The duties of an escort to a lady are manifold and various, and the true lady will make them as light as possible, striving, by her own deportment and agreeable conversation, to compensate her gentleman friend for the trouble she may occasion him. To weary him constantly by complaints of the heat, dust, or flies; to worry for half an hour over some unavoidable mishap or annoyance; to lose or miss some part of her hand-baggage every five minutes; forcing him to rise and search for what she eventually finds in her own pocket; to inquire every few moments, "Where are we now? what time is it? are we nearly at our journey's end?" to delay him, when the train or boat does stop, for arrangements that should have been made ten minutes before; to fidget about her baggage; or to find constant fault with what he cannot control, are all faults in which lady travellers are prone to indulge, but which all mark low breeding, founded upon intense selfishness. Good-nature, perfect courtesy, patience, punctuality, and an easy adaptation to perhaps untoward circumstances mark the perfect lady in travelling. When you see a lady, detained perhaps for hours by a snow-storm, pleasantly trying to beguile the time by conversation, relieving tired mothers, perhaps, of the care of fretful children, jesting pleasantly upon the unpleasant delay, and uttering no complaint or impatient word, even if half frozen or in utter discomfort, you may be certain you see a perfectly well-bred lady in every sense of the words.

No lady should ever allow her escort to enter with her any saloon devoted exclusively to the use of ladies. Because he may be her own husband, son, father, or brother does not excuse her, as he cannot stand in such relation to others present.

If a lady in a car or stage finds the exertion of talking tiresome or painful, she may say so frankly, and no gentleman must take offence. Weak lungs may be really injured by the effort made to be heard above the noise of a locomotive or wheels.

In travelling alone, a lady should speak to the conductor on a train, or, in a long steamer passage, introduce herself to the captain, explaining her unprotected situation, and they are bound to extend every courtesy in their power. It is better for a lady so travelling to wait until the rush of passengers is over before quitting a train or boat, and then, if not waiting to meet any one, leave the station.

A lady travelling alone may, with perfect propriety, accept courtesy from strange gentlemen, such as raising or lowering a window, the offer of a hand across a slippery plank, or any such attention, being careful always to thank him politely for the same, and in a tone that will not encourage conversation or further advances.

Any apology made during a journey for accidental crushing, crowding, reaching over the seat, or the like, must be accepted, a silent but courteous bow being the best acknowledment of the politeness dictating such apology.

A gentleman, on entering a public carriage or omnibus, must never step before a lady, but stand aside until she enters, raising the hat slightly if she acknowledges his courtesy, as a true lady will, by a bow. He may offer to assist her if she appears to need it, even if she is a perfect stranger to him.

If a gentleman consents to act as escort to a lady, he must carefully fulfill all the requirements of that rather arduous position. If she meets him at a wharf or depôt, he must be a little before the hour for starting, to procure her ticket, check her baggage, and secure for her a pleasant seat. He must never leave her to stand in an office or upon a wharf whilst he attends to her tickets and baggage; but, having seen her comfortably seated in a ladies' room or cabin, return for those duties. In arriving at a station, he must see her seated in a hack before he attends to the trunks.

In a hotel, the gentleman must escort the lady to the parlor before securing her room, but not detain her afterwards. However agreeable she may be, he may be certain she is longing to rest after her journey, and remove the travel stains from her face and dress. He must at once escort her to her room, ascertain what hour it will be agreeable for her take the next meal, and meet her again in the parlor at that hour. He must not leave her upon arriving at the journey's end until he has escorted her to the house, and if he remains in the city, he must call the next day to inquire after her health. After that, the lady may continue the acquaintance or not, as she pleases; but if she declines to do so, by non-recognition at the next meeting, he is at liberty to decline acting in the capacity of escort to her again.

A gentleman who is travelling alone may offer little courtesies to strangers, and even to ladies, carefully maintaining a respectful manner, that may assure them they need not fear to encourage impertinence by accepting the proferred civilities.

In travelling abroad, the truest courtesy is to observe as far as practicable every national prejudice. The old proverb, to "do in Rome as Romans do," is the best rule of etiquette in foreign travel. The man who affects a supercilious disdain for all foreign customs and forms will not convince the natives of his vast superiority, but impress them with the belief that he is an ill-bred idiot. The most polite, as well as agreeable travellers are those who will smilingly devour mouse-pie and bird's-nest soup in China, dine contentedly upon horse-steak in Paris, swallow their beef uncooked in Germany, maintain an unwinking gravity over the hottest curry in India, smoke their hookah gratefully in Turkey, mount an elephant in Ceylon, and, in short, conform gracefully to any native custom, however strange it may appear to him.

"Comparisons are odious," and to be continually asserting that everything in the United States is vastly superior to everything abroad is a mark of vulgarity. If you really think there is nothing to be seen abroad as good as you have at home, why, you are foolish not to stay at home and enjoy the best.

A lady may, under certain circumstances, as, if she be a married lady, and not too young, begin a conversation with a strange gentlemen; but he must not, under any circumstances, begin a conversation with her. An unmarried lady, unless advanced in life, is not supposed to begin conversation with a strange gentleman.

When a lady, travelling alone, wishes to descend from a railway car, it is the duty of the gentleman nearest the door to assist her in alighting, even if he resumes his seat again. He may offer to collect her baggage, call a hack, or perform any service her escort would have attended to.

If a train stop for refreshments, a gentleman may, with perfect propriety, offer to escort a strange lady, who is alone, to the refreshment-room, or to bring to her any refreshments she may desire. If she accepts his offer, he must see that she is served with all that she desires before attending to his own wants. A lady may always accept such an offer of attention, thanking the gentleman for his politeness, and dismissing him by a courteous bow, which he must accept as an intimation that his services are no longer required.

Smoking in the presence of ladies is uncourteous, even if there is no law against it in the car, stage, or boat. Some smokers, of more inveterate weakness in the direction of tobacco than of strength in politeness, make a parade of asking the permission of any lady who may be present; but this is hardly enough. A lady will not like to refuse, although she may dislike the smoke, and she ought not to be put to her election between two alternatives almost equally disagreeable. If gentlemen only are present, the question should be put to each and every one of them whether they have any objection to smoking in their presence. One dissentient voice should carry the day; for no gentleman has a right to insist upon his own special gratification if it will cause annoyance and discomfort to others present. Should there be no objection on the part of the entire party, the gentleman who first strikes his fusee should offer it to any others near him about to indulge also before he uses it himself.

As regards the right to have the window up or down, the person who sits facing the the engine has the command. Ladies, being present, should, of course, be consulted, no matter on which side they may be sitting, and their wish must be considered a final settlement of the question.

If a gentleman have any newspapers, he must offer them first to his travelling companions. If refused, he may use them himself, thus leaving them free to read also if they so desire.

ETIQUETTE IN CHURCH.

In visiting a church in which you have no pew of your own, wait in the vestibule until the sexton comes to you, and request him to show you to a seat. It is extremely rude to enter a pew without invitation if it is partially filled, or without permission if it is empty.

Always enter a church slowly and reverentially. A gentleman must remove his hat at the door, and never replace it until he is again in the vestibule.

Conform strictly to the forms of worship. If you are not familiar with them, rise, kneel, and sit as you see others do.

Never whisper to a companion in church.

Never make any noise with your feet or fingers.

Never stare round the building.

Never bow to any friend while in the church itself. Greetings may be exchanged in the vestibule after service.

A gentleman accompanying a lady to a Roman Catholic church, even if himself a Protestant, may offer her the holy water, and it must be with an ungloved hand.

Gentlemen must pass up the aisle beside their lady companions until they reach the pew, then advance a few steps, open the door, and stand aside until she has entered, then enter, and close the door again. It is a bad plan to leave the hat outside, as it is liable to be swept down the aisle by the skirts of ladies passing. If there is not room for it on the seat, it can be put upon the floor inside the pew.

Never pay any attention to those around you, even if they are noisy or rude.

If you pass a book or a fan to a person in the same pew, or accept the same attention, it is not necessary to speak. A silent bow is all that etiquette requires.

If you have room in your own pew, and see a stranger enter, open the door and motion him to enter. It is not necessary to speak.

You may find the place and point it out to a stranger, who is unfamiliar with the service; but do so silently.

A lady should never remove her gloves in church, unless to use the holy water, or the right-hand glove at communion.

To come late to church is not only ill-bred, but disrespectful. It is equally so to hurry away, or to commence preparations for departure, closing and putting away the books, and such preparations, before the service closes.

Never keep any one waiting if you are invited or have invited them to go to church.

When visiting a church abroad, not to attend divine service, but to see the edifice, choose an hour when there is no service. If you find worshippers, however, are present, move quietly, speak low, and endeavor not to disturb their devotions.

The godmother at a christening must accompany the family of her little godchild to and from the church, and should send her gift (usually a silver cup) the day before.

In attending a funeral not in your own family, never leave the pew until the mourners have passed into the aisle; but rise and stand while they pass, falling into your proper place as the procession passes you.

It is ill-bred for gentlemen to congregate in the vestibule of a church and there chat familiarly, often commenting audibly upon the service or the congregation. No true lady likes to run this gauntlet, although in this country they are too often obliged to do so.

To show any disrespect to a form of worship that may be new or strange to you is rude in the extreme. If you find it trying to your own religious convictions, you need not again visit churches of the same denomination; but to sneer at a form, while in the church using that form, is insulting and low-bred.

ETIQUETTE FOR PLACES OF AMUSEMENT.

A gentleman who wishes to invite a young lady, who is not related to him, to visit any place of public amusement with him, must, the first time that he invites her, also invite another lady of the same family to accompany her. No young lady should visit public places of amusement with a gentleman with whom she is but slightly acquainted, alone.

It is a gentleman's duty to invite a lady long enough before the evening of the performance to be certain of securing pleasant seats, as it is but a poor compliment to take her where she will be uncomfortable, or where she can neither hear nor see.

Although a carriage may not be necessary on account of the weather, it is a more elegant way of paying attention to a lady to provide one.

Never assume an air of secrecy or mystery in a public place; and even if you have the right to do so, assume no lover-like airs. It is rude to converse loudly, especially during the performance; but a low tone is all that is necessary; not a whisper.

To appear to comment aside upon those near you is extremely ill-bred.

A lady is not expected to bow to a friend across a theatre or concert-room; but a gentleman may recognize his lady friends.

A lady must answer a note of invitation to visit a place of public amusement as soon as possible, as, by delay, she may keep her gentleman friend in doubt, and deprive him of the pleasure of inviting another friend if she declines.

It is ill-bred to arrive late at any public entertainment, and looks as if you were not sufficiently master of your own time to be punctual.

In a theatre, give your attention entirely to the stage when the curtain is up; to your companion when it is down.

It looks badly to see a lady staring round the house with an opera-glass. Never is a modest dignity more becoming than in a theatre. To indulge in extravagant gesture, laugh boisterously, flirt a fan conspicuously, toy with an eye-glass or opera-glass, indulge in lounging attitudes, whisper aside, are all unlady-like in the extreme.

If you speak to your companion during the performance, do so in a low tone, that you may not disturb those who are near you, and wish to hear the actors.

In entering a concert-room or the box of a theatre, a gentleman should precede a lady, if there is not room to walk beside her, until they reach the seats, then hand her to the inner one, taking the outside one himself. In going out, if he cannot offer her his arm, he must again walk before her, until he reaches the lobby, and then offer her his arm.

Boisterous applause and loud laughter are ungentlemanly.

It is in bad taste to distract your companion's interest from the performance, even if you find it dull yourself.

No gentleman should leave a lady alone for a moment in a public place of amusement. He may subject her to annoyance, or he may find another lady in his seat when he returns, which would separate him from his companion until the close of the performance; for, although a gentleman when alone should offer his seat to a lady or old gentleman who cannot procure one, he is not expected to do so when escorting a lady. His place is then that of protector to his charge, and he must not relinquish it for a moment.

Secure a libretto, or programme, before taking your seat, that you may not be obliged to rise to get one.

At the opera, conversation during the performance is in the worst taste. The lowest tone will disturb the real lovers of music. Exclamations of "Lovely!" "Exquisite!" "How sweet!" and others, are all proofs of vulgarity.

If you promenade at a concert or between the acts at a theatre, you may bow to friends the first time you pass them only. A lady must not allow other gentlemen to join her, if she would not offend her escort, and no gentleman will stop a lady to speak to her. A conversation of a moment or two is all that is allowable in such meetings.

If seats are secured, it is best to arrive about five minutes before the commencement of a performance; but if a gentleman is escorting a lady to an entertainment where seats cannot be secured, he should call for her at an early hour, that she may get a good place.

In a picture-gallery, never stand conversing before the paintings in such a way as to interrupt the view of others. If you wish to converse, stand aside or take seats and do so.

A gentleman alone may join lady friends for a few moments between the acts at a theatre, or in the intermission at a concert, but only for a few moments, as their escort has a prior claim upon their attention.

It is an act of rudeness to join any party about to visit a place of amusement, or at one, unless urgently invited, and no one of taste will ever form a third. If two or three ladies are in the party and but one gentleman, another gentleman, if well acquainted, may offer his services as escort to one of the ladies, and if not allowed to share the expenses, should invite the party to partake of refreshments after the performance is over.

Always enter a concert-hall or lecture-room as quietly as possible

Never push violently through a crowd at a public place. A lady will always find room made for her if she requests it, or if it is requested by her escort.

After escorting a lady to a place of amusement, a gentleman may ask permission to call the following morning or evening, and the lady must be at home to receive that call. She should take that opportunity to thank him for the pleasure she has enjoyed, and find some warm words of praise for the performance. To severely criticize on such an occasion is rude to the escort, who has intended to give pleasure, and the performance must be bad indeed where nothing can be found to merit a word of praise.

In visiting a fancy fair, too many persons act as if they were in a store, cheapening the articles offered for sale, and being careless about their criticisms and remarks. It is impossible to tell who may be wounded by such conduct. The very lady who offers you an article you pronounce "absolutely hideous" may have spent hours in its manufacture, and feel proportionately hurt at your remarks. Courtesy and words of praise are never more appreciated than by those who have spent weary hours in preparing for this most troublesome of all charities.

On the other hand, the position of a lady at the table of a fancy fair is necessarily an exposed one, and requires a great amount of modest dignity to support it. Flirting, loud talking, importunate entreaties to unwilling friends to buy your goods, are all in bad taste; and it is equally bad to leave your place every few moments to visit the refreshment-table in company with your gentlemen friends. We heard a lady boast once that she had been seventeen times in one day to the refreshment-table "for the good of the fair," and we could not but think the cause might have been aided without quite such a display of gastronomic energy. No true lady will follow friends all around the room offering goods for sale, nor force articles on reluctant purchasers by appealing to their gallantry.

In entering a fancy fair where many ladies are present, strict etiquette requires a gentleman to remove his hat, and carry it whilst in the room, but it is a rule much neglected.

It is rude for a lady to take advantage of the rule which prevents a gentleman from asking for change at a fair. If he says, in presenting a larger amount than the purchased article calls for, "Pray accept the balance for the object for which you are working," she may, of course, place the gift in her cash-box; otherwise it is more lady-like to give back the change.

SERVANTS.

It would be difficult to express the sense of etiquette on this subject better than by quoting Lord Chesterfield's words:

"I am more upon my guard," he writes, "as to my behavior to my servants and to others who are called my inferiors than I am towards my equals, for fear of being suspected of that mean and ungenerous sentiment of desiring to make others feel that difference which fortune has, and perhaps too undeservedly, made between us."

Conduct towards servants should be always equal, never violent, never familiar. Speak to them always with civility, but keep them in their proper places.

Give no occasion for them to complain of you; but never suffer yourself to complain of them without first ascertaining that your complaint is just, seeing that it has attention, and that the fault complained of is remedied.

Beware of giving servants the inch; there is no class so prone, under such circumstances, to take the ell.

If staying in a friend's house, you may assume, to a certain extent, that your friend's servants are your servants. But this must be only so far as you are yourself concerned. You must not, on any account, give directions respecting the general conduct of the *ménage*. For all your own personal wants, however, you are free to command their services. Ask for anything, under their control, that may be lacking in your own room; for whatever you need at meal times; let them call you in the morning if you sleep soundly; do not send them on errands, however, without first ascertaining that it will not interfere with their regular routine of household duty; but do anything and everything required for your own personal convenience and comfort through the servants. It is contrary to all laws of etiquette to trouble your host or hostess with all your petty wants.

Never apologize for the trouble you give them; but if you should, through illness or other cause, occasion more work than a visitor ordinarily brings to a household, let the gift, which, in any case, you would make to the servants on leaving the house, be somewhat heavier than would otherwise have been necessary.

This question of fees to servants is a very important one. Many people are disposed to regard it as an imposition which is tolerated only through the force of custom. Others view it in the light of paying for an extra burden, which their presence has laid upon the servant's shoulders. The latter view, if not entirely the correct one, is, at least, as reasonable as the former, and a generous nature will probably adopt it. The opposition will say, "But all cannot afford to make these presents," and "The servants are hired on the express understanding that they will have to serve their employer's guests, as part of the work they are engaged to do." There is something in this; but, on the other hand, it might be asked, "Do any of you who complain of having to make these involuntary gifts for extra service on the part of the servants, rest satisfied in your own minds when your profession, business, or the service from which you draw your source of living, requires extra exertions from you?" You are, perhaps, the manager of the greatest bank that ever was opened, or the director of the largest department under the control of the State. Do you not, when anything more than usual is required of you, look for, if you do not get, extra remuneration, in the shape of promotion, money, or testimonials? I am sure you do, if you would speak honestly, and, if so, how can you suppose servants should expect otherwise? Whether they get all they look for, or think they ought to have, is a separate affair. Perhaps you, too, do not get all you deem yourself to merit. The system of fees is, no doubt, like all other human institutions, liable to considerable abuse. At one time it was considered beneath the dignity of a gentleman to give anything but gold, and whilst that superstition prevailed, it must doubtless have pressed very hard upon poor people, to whom to go into society was to be ruinously fined, without the privilege of appeal. Even at the present day, there are certain classes of servants who are "as death, and cannot be satisfied," unless their "itching palms" are heavily laden with their fee; but they are but rarely approached by poorer people.

With regard to the amount of fees to servants in a household, it is not possible to lay down any precise rule. Much must depend on the length of the visit, the position of the master of the house, and the position in which you are supposed to stand toward him; and on each of these points you must exercise your own discretion, and consult your own means or generosity.

Gentlemen give fees to the men servants only, as a general rule, and ladies give to the female servants only; and though the strict observance of this rule may seem at times to work injustice, it is better to adhere to it than to mar the comfort and position of those who come after you, and who may not have the means of being liberal over and above the prescribed standard. Under no circumstances is a lady called upon by the rules of etiquette to give fees to men servants; the lady's-maid and the housemaid are the only ones she is expected to remember; but if a gentleman visit where only female servants are employed, he should make them a present on his departure.

Feeing the servants in a hotel is open to many objections, as it is apt to influence them unduly in second or third arrivals at the same house; but it is a custom so fixed that it has become second nature to them to look for it. It is certainly a person's own fault if he submits to being fleeced by the servants in a hotel. Attendance is certainly included in the high prices charged, yet the custom prevails in spite of it, and those who do not comply with it will soon find the difference, although there may be nothing sufficiently impertinent or negligent for positive complaint.

Fees to railway porters and others are certainly not required by the rules of etiquette to be paid. The payment of them is indeed forbidden by many of the railway companies; but the receiving of them is winked at, the result being that travellers who want attendance are, for the most part, obliged to pay for it. The system is, however, a pernicious one, and travellers should discourage it as much as possible, if only for the sake of those who cannot afford to sustain it.

"I am sorry," said a gentleman to a porter (need we say an Irishman?) who had looked after a number of parcels, and stowed them conveniently away in the car, "that the regulations of the company do not allow me to give you a shilling." "If your honor," replied the porter, with a grin, "were to lose *two*, I should know where to find them."

At a dinner party, an evening company, a ball, or like occasions, it is customary, on coming away, to give a trifle, the gentleman to the waiter who hands him his hat, etc., the lady to the attendant in the dressing-room; but you are not called upon to remember every servant in attendance. There is a story told of an old English gentleman, rich enough to be above the suggestion of poverty, and notoriously liberal enough to be above the imputation of meanness, who, being at a dinner party, was presented by one servant with his hat. To this man he gave a shilling. Another advanced, and helped him into his coat, and to him the old gentleman also gave a shilling. A third gave him his cane, and received in exchange a shilling; but when a fourth approached, bearing his gloves, the old gentleman gazed upon him for a moment, and then said, quietly: "You may keep them, my good man; it will be cheaper for me than to receive them," and then walked out. This was, however, an abuse of advantage on the part of the servants, which, if repeated, others would do well to rebuke in a similar manner.

An English writer on this subject gives some hints that would be equally conducive to regularity and comfort if adopted in this country, saying:

"There is no question but that we should seek to perform *all* our duties without hope of recompense; and yet, as regards our treatment of servants, we should be especially careful that, in endeavoring to make their bodily comfort and mental improvement an object of consideration, we do not allow ourselves to dwell upon the hope of gratitude or affection from them in return. Many have done so, and having, with that view, been tempted to accord unwise indulgences and to overlook serious faults, they have found that, far from gaining the love of their servants, they have incurred their contempt; and when they have perceived that their favors, unappreciated, have led but to new encroachments, they have hardened their hearts, and rushed into an opposite extreme. Then they have considered their servants as mere machines, from which labor must be extorted by all available means.

"A man-servant is rarely grateful, and seldom attached. He is generally incapable of appreciating those advantages which, with your cultivated judgment, you know to be most conducive to his welfare. Do you accord to him regular hours, and a stated allowance of work; do you refrain from sending him out because it is wet, and he is unwell; do you serve yourself rather than ring for him at dinner time, he will rarely have the grace to thank you in his heart for your constant consideration. Hear him. He will thus describe a comfortable place: 'There were very few in the family; when they went out of a night, we made it up in the morning; we had nice hot suppers, and the cook made a good hash for breakfast, and we always get luncheon between that and dinner; and we were all very comfortable together, and had a friend in when we liked. Master swore at us sometimes, but often made us a present for it when he had been very violent; a good-hearted man as ever lived, and mistress was quite the lady, and never meddled with servants. It was a capital place.'

"Servants' sympathies are with their equals. They feel for a poor servant run off his legs, and moped to death; they have no feeling for a painstaking mistress, economical both from principle and scanty means; they would (most of them) see her property wasted, and her confidence abused without compunction. It is the last effort of virtue in a servant if, without any ***private reason,*** he should discharge his duty by informing you of the injury which you are enduring at the hands of his fellow-servant. It is an effort of virtue; for it will bring down many a bitter taunt and hard word upon his faithful head.

"'I never got a servant out of a place by telling tales on him,' will be said to him. Directly a servant departs, we all know, tongues tied before are loosened to gain our favor by apparent candor. When it can avail us nothing, we are told. We all know this, and have said: 'Be silent now; you should have mentioned this to me at the time it occurred.'

"Supposing, then, you have the *rara avis,* the servant that 'speaks at the time,' be chary of him—or let me say *her* (the best servants are women). Oh! as you value her, let her not suppose you cannot part with her. Treat her with confidence, but with strict impartiality; reprove where necessary, mildly, but decidedly, lest she should presume (power is so tempting), and compel you, if you would retain your freedom, to let her go.

"There is one thing a man-servant values beyond all that your kindness and consideration can do for him—his liberty; liberty to eat, drink, and be merry, with your things, in the company of his own friends; liberty to get the housemaid to clean his candlesticks and bring up his coals; and the housemaid wishes for liberty to lie in bed in the morning, because she was up so late talking to John in the pantry; liberty to wear flounces and flowers. The cook desires liberty too. For this liberty, if you grant it, they will despise you; if you deny it, they will respect you. Aim at their esteem; despair of their love or gratitude; make your place what the best class of servants will value, and, though in their heart they may not thank you for it, you will gain, perhaps, one servant out of twenty who will keep gross imposition and gross immorality at bay.

"These remarks can never be intended to deny the warm attachment of female servants to the children of their employers. Deep love, no doubt, is lavished by many a woman on the babe she has nursed. There is a great deal to be said on the chapter of nurses, which would require to be dealt with by itself. Much wisdom is required in the administration of a nursery, to which but few general rules would apply. Cruel is the tyranny the nurse frequently practises on the parent, who often refrains from entering her nursery, not from want of love for her children, but positive dread of the sour looks which greet her. Let her be firm; let no shrinking from grieving her darling, who would 'break his heart if his Nana went,' deter her from discharging the encroaching servant.

"On the choice of servants much of the comfort of the young housekeeper depends. It often happens that her choice has been determined by appearance rather than the value of character. If such be the case, she will have many difficulties to encounter. It is, in the present day, hardly safe to take a servant if there be a single objection to character, however it may be glossed over by the person referred to on this point; for there is now an unhealthy disposition to pass over the failings of servants who have left their places, and to make them perfect in the eyes of others. In respect to sobriety, many people will not acknowledge that a servant had had the vice of drinking, but will cover the unpleasant truth with such gentle and plausible terms that it becomes difficult to comprehend how far the hint is grounded, or not. Be assured when a lady or gentleman hesitates on this point, or on that of honesty, it is wiser not to engage a servant. Nor are you deviating from Christian charity in not overlooking a dereliction of so material a sort. The kindest plan to the vast community of domestic servants is to be rigid in all important points, and, having, after a due experience, a just confidence in them, to be somewhat more indulgent to errors of a more trivial nature.

"It is always desirable to have, if possible, servants of one faith But if it so happens that you have a Roman Catholic servant and a Protestant in your service, you are bound to allow each the free exercise of her religion, and you ought not to respect them if, out of interest, they will conform to yours. An exercise of authority on this point amounts, in my opinion, to an act of tyranny, and it can only tend to promote insincerity, and, perhaps, engender skepticism in its object. Nothing is, indeed, so dangerous as to unsettle the faith of the lower classes, who have neither time nor opportunity of fairly considering subjects of religious controversy.

"While on the subject of servants, I must deprecate the over-indulgence of the present system towards them. Formerly they were treated with real kindness; but it was the kindness that exacted duty in return, and took a real interest in the welfare of each servant. The reciprocal tie in former times between servant and master was strong; now it is wholly gone. The easy rule of masters and mistresses proceeds far more from indifference than from kindness of heart; for the real charity is to keep servants steadily to their duties. They are a class of persons to whom much leisure is destruction; the pursuits of their idle hours are seldom advantageous to them, and theirs are not minds, generally, which can thrive in repose. Idleness, to them, is peculiarly the root of all evil; for if their time is not spent in vicious amusements, it is often passed in scandal, discontent, and vanity. In writing thus, I do not recommend a hard or inconsiderate system to servants. They require, and in many instances they merit, all that can be done to alleviate a situation of servitude. They ought not to be the slaves of caprice or the victims of temper. Their work should be measured out with a just hand; but it should be regularly exacted in as much perfection as can be expected in variable and erring human nature.

"Another point on which I would recommend firmness is that of early hours. In this respect, example is as important as precept; but, however uncertain you may be yourself, I would not relax a rule of this kind; for every comfort during the day depends on the early rising of your servants. Without this, all their several departments are hurried through or neglected in some important respect.

"Your mode of address to servants must be decisive, yet mild. The authoritative tone I do not recommend. It is very unbecoming to any young person, and it rarely attains the end desired; but there is a quiet dignity of deportment which few servants ever can resist. This should be tempered with kindness, when circumstances call it forth, but should never descend to familiarity; for no caution is more truly kind than that which confines servants strictly to their own sphere.

"Much evil results from the tendency, more especially of the very young or of very old mistresses of families, to partiality. Commonly, one servant becomes the almost avowed favorite; and it is difficult to say whether that display of partiality is the more pernicious to the servant who is the object of it, or to the rankling and jealous minds of the rest of the household. It is true that it is quite impossible to avoid entertaining a greater degree of confidence in some servants than in others; but it should be shown with a due regard to the feelings of all. It is, of course, allowable towards those who take a decidedly responsible and confidential situation in a household. Still, never let such persons assume the reins of government; let them act the part of helmsmen to the vessel, but not aspire to the control of the captain.

"It is generally wise and right, after a due experience of the principles and intentions of servants, to place confidence in their honesty, and to let them have the comfort of knowing that you do so. At the same time, never cease to exercise a system of supervision. The great principle of housekeeping is regularity, and without this (one of the most difficult of the minor virtues to practise), all efforts to promote order must be ineffectual. I have seen energetic women, clever and well-intentioned, fail in attaining a good method, owing to their being uncertain in hours, governed by impulse, and capricious. I have seen women, inferior in capacity, slow, and apathetic, make excellent heads of families, as far as their household was concerned, from their steadiness and regularity. Their very power of enduring monotony has been favorable to their success in this way, especially if they are not called upon to act in peculiar and difficult cases, in which their actual inferiority is traceable. But these are not the ordinary circumstances of life."

In this country, servants are proverbially more troublesome than in Europe, where service is often transmitted through generations in one family. Here, the housekeeper is obliged to change often, taking frequently the most ignorant of the lower classes of foreigners to train into good and useful servants, only to have them become dissatisfied as soon as they become acquainted with others, who instil the republican doctrine of perfect equality into their minds, ruining them for good servants. There are some points of etiquette, however, upon which every lady should insist:

Never allow a servant to keep people waiting upon the doorstep.

Never allow servants to treat any one disrespectfully.

Never allow servants to turn their own proper duties over to the children or other servants by a bribe. Many fond parents would be amazed if they knew how much running and actual work was performed by little Nellie or Charlie, and how many fits of mysterious indigestion were caused by the rich cake, candy, or half-ripe fruit that paid for the service and bribed the silence.

Never allow a servant to keep a visitor standing parleying on the door-step, while she holds the door ajar. Train the door-servant to admit any caller promptly, show them to the parlor, bring up their cards at once, and return with your answer or message.

There are two occasions in a man's lifetime when may he make his account with liberality to servants, whether he will or whether he will not. These two are the occasions of his marriage and his funeral.

On his marriage, the bridegroom is expected to make presents to all the servants of his father-in-law or mother-in-law, rather according to their expectations than according to his means. To old servants, who have been attached to the bride, the bridegroom will naturally wish to give some token of the value he sets upon their devotion. New dresses, new shawls, money, or a handsome equivalent of it, are expected. Money is usually given to the other servants. The amounts must, of course, depend, in a great degree, upon the means of the bridegroom; but he must be prepared for a heavy outlay on the occasion, if the servants be numerous.

HOTEL ETIQUETTE.

Let us start this chapter by saying that no word of it is addressed to the sterner sex, who will find hints for their etiquette under the head of "Travelling;" but it is for the especial guidance of ladies, many of whom in this independent country travel without escort.

When a lady arrives alone at a hotel, she should, if possible, be provided with a letter of introduction to the proprietor; she should send for him immediately upon her arrival, present her letter, or her card, and mention the time for which she desires to secure a room.

In going to meals, a lady should request one of the waiters to meet her at the dining-room door, and escort her to the table, saving her the awkwardness of crossing the room alone, and showing others that she is a regular resident in the house. She may keep the services of this waiter at table during her stay, and should give him a present of money before leaving.

In giving an order at a public table, a lady should decide quickly what dishes she desires, and order them in a low but distinct tone.

No lady will stare round the room, fidget with her napkin, plate, knife, or fork, play with the salt, or exhibit any awkward embarrassment, while waiting for a meal to be served. It is allowable to look over a newspaper in the interval at breakfast; but the habit, quite common, of carrying a novel to the table is not lady-like.

If a lady accepts any civility from a gentleman at the same table, such as placing butter, sugar, or water nearer to her plate, she must thank him; but by no means start a conversation with him.

If a lady have friends at the table, she may converse in a low, quiet tone; but any loud tone, laughing extravagantly, or gesticulations, are exceedingly ill-bred. To comment upon others present, either aloud or in a whisper, is extremely rude.

A lady must never point to any dish she wishes passed to her. If she cannot call it by name, a well-trained waiter will know her wishes if she looks at the dish.

Any bold action or boisterous deportment in a hotel will expose a lady to the most severe censure of the refined around her, and may render her liable to misconstruction, and impertinence.

Greetings offered by other ladies at the table, or in the parlor, should not be too hastily checked, as the acquaintance so formed is never required by etiquette to be recognized elsewhere.

A lady alone at a hotel should wear the most modest and least conspicuous dress appropriate to the hour of the day. Full dress must not be worn unless she has an escort present.

A lady should never go alone to the supper-table after ten o'clock. If she returns from an entertainment at a later hour, and has no escort to supper, she should have that meal sent to her room.

A lady should carefully lock her trunks before leaving her room at a hotel, and should give her purse and jewelry into the care of the proprietor on her arrival, ringing for them if she requires them during her stay.

No lady should open a window in a hotel parlor, if there are other ladies near it, without first ascertaining that it will not inconvenience them.

No lady should use the piano of a hotel uninvited if there are others in the room. It looks bold and forward to display even the most finished musical education in this way. It is still worse to sing.

A lady should never go herself to the door of a hotel to call a hack. Ring for a servant to perform this office, and he will bring the hack to the ladies' entrance.

No lady should stand or linger in the halls of a hotel, but pass through them quietly, never stopping alone for a moment.

No lady should stand alone at the front windows of a hotel parlor, nor may she walk out on the porch, or, indeed, any conspicuous place.

A lady is not expected to recognize her friends across the parlor or dining-room of a hotel.

No scolding of servants is permissible in a hotel. If they are negligent or disrespectful, complain to the housekeeper or landlord; it is their business to keep the domestics in order, not that of their guests.

For a lady to go up the stairs of a hotel singing is ill-bred, and may expose her to rudeness.

It is a breach of etiquette to take any newspaper, book, or music you may find in a hotel parlor to your own room, even if you return it.

Lolling or lounging in a public parlor can never be permitted to a lady.

It is a breach of etiquette for a lady to touch her baggage in a hotel after it is packed. There are plenty of servants to attend to it, and they should carry to the hack even the travelling-shawl, satchel, and railway novel. Nothing looks more awkward than to see a lady, with both hands full, stumbling up the steps of a hotel hack.

No lady must ever pass in or out at the public entrance of a hotel. There is always an entrance for ladies especially, and it is bold and unbecoming for them to be seen in the one appropriated to gentlemen. A gentleman who will escort a lady through the public entrance shows a lamentable ignorance of the usages of hotel life.

WEDDING ETIQUETTE.

To those who require to be taught how they may express themselves in those delicate negotiations which precede the question of marriage, this little book is not addressed. It is not proposed to introduce form and ceremony into that which should spring purely and spontaneously from the heart, and which should be the most natural expression of a most natural feeling, in connection with which etiquette would be simply a mockery. Etiquette, being only a system devised and found convenient for the social rule and guidance of the many, cannot by any possibility be applied to the conduct of two who may reasonably be supposed to be acquainted with each other's sentiments before they begin to speak about them. If they are not so acquainted, all the etiquette in the world cannot help them, nor preserve them from making what may be a blunder of the most awkward kind. There are people who profess to teach how and in what terms an offer of marriage should be made, whether by letter or by mouth, and, in either case, what should be said. I pretend to no such knowledge, believing that if the heart cannot suggest the way and the words, nothing else can do so.

Yet, the wiser way, usually, is in speech. Letters are seldom expressive of what really passes in the mind of a man; or, if expressive, seem foolish, since deep feelings are liable to exaggeration. Every written word may be the theme of cavil. Study, care, which avail in every other species of composition, are death to the lover's effusion. A few sentences, spoken in earnest, and broken by emotion, are more eloquent than pages of sentiment, both to parents and daughter.

The place of etiquette, the social law which regulates the conduct of engaged people towards others, and of other people towards them, is immediately after the announcement of the engagement; then there is scope for the display of good manners and good breeding, and there are certain rules which must be observed.

Some members of the gentleman's family, his nearest relations, should call upon the family of the lady, and they should return the call as soon as possible. It is by no means necessary that the two families should be intimate; there may be good and sufficient reasons why they should not be so; all that is necessary is the show of civility, which is included in the interchange of visits. If the family of the gentleman does not reside in the same city as that of the lady, the announcement of the engagement should be followed by letters from his parents or nearest relatives to the young lady herself or her parents. Kindly and cordial feeling should be the prevailing tone of such letters, and they must be answered at once.

Though it is often true that the gentleman who aspires to love one member of a family must make his account in loving all the rest in some degree, there is no necessity for such a display of amiability on the part of the lady.

It is customary for the gentleman to make some present to his fiancée soon after the engagement. The most elegant and desirable present is a handsome ring, "the engagement ring," which should be either of diamonds or pearls. The lady sometimes returns a similar ring, or the gentleman has two made exactly similar, each of the betrothed wearing one.

The first present must be made by the gentleman. It is very proper for this first present to be followed by gifts upon appointed days, as birthdays, Christmas, or New Year's Day, and the lady is at perfect liberty to return the compliment. It is considered more elegant for the gentleman to offer jewelry, the lady some gift which is the work of her own hands, as a handsome pair of embroidered slippers, a handkerchief with richly embroidered monograms, a cigar-case embroidered, or some similar gift.

When once the engagement is allowed, it is the custom to admit the gentleman into the intimate society of his newly-adopted relatives; he is looked upon as something more than a potential member of the family; he is implicitly trusted in every way.

It is a gross breach of good manners to omit the gentleman from any invitation in which his fiancée is included, and there are not many young ladies who would consent to accept such an invitation. There is, however, no rule of etiquette forbidding an engaged lady to do so, if she so desires.

In return for the membership which is accorded to him in the lady's family, the engaged man should show all possible deference towards the of members it, especially to the parents. Towards the sisters of his lady love, he should be kind; and generally attentive, and frank, and cordial in his intercourse with her brothers. If there are young children in the family, nothing will make him more popular with the older members than an occasional gift of toys or confectionery, or an excursion during the holidays with the schoolboys, who will readily swear allegiance, after such a trip, to "the man Emily is going to marry," or (vulgar little wretches that they are) to "Amelia's *beau*."

It is not according to the strict laws of etiquette for the brothers and sisters to call the new member at first by his Christian name. Much will depend on his age and his disposition. There are some people whom one can never address otherwise than formally, while with others it seems perfect nonsense to call them otherwise than by the most familiar term.

If not a positive requirement of etiquette, it is, at least, a politic thing to pay considerable attention to the future mother-in-law. To occupy a good place in her esteem and affection is to smooth many a furrow, which otherwise might trip one up in his walk over the tender ground that leads to matrimony.

An engaged man should never forget the exceedingly abnormal position he occupies with reference to the lady's family; the inconvenience his presence may occasion, and the amount of forbearance necessary on their parts to insure even a friendly status for him in the household. He should endeavor to repay this by a careful attention to the general rules of the family, and even to the particular fancies of the members; he should rigidly observe their hours for meals, and be careful not to stay later in the evening than the usual hour for the household to retire.

There should be the most perfect candor, on the gentleman's part, concerning the state of his financial affairs, and he should respectfully consider the worldly position of the family he is to enter, never doing anything to hurt their feelings, either by word or act, should their status be below his own, and never professing scorn or contempt for wealth or power, should their status be higher than his own.

During the arrangement of pecuniary matters, a young lady should endeavor to understand what is going on, receiving it in a right spirit. If she has a private fortune, she should, in all points left to her, be generous and confiding; at the same time, prudent. Many a man, she should remember, may abound in excellent qualities, and yet be improvident. He may mean to do well, yet have a passion for building; he may be the very soul of good-nature, yet be fond of the gaming-table; he may have no wrong propensities, and yet have a confused notion of accounts, and be one of those unfortunate men who muddle away a great deal of money, no one knows how; or he may be a too strict economist, a man who takes too good care of the pence, till he tires his wife's life out about an extra dollar; or he may be facile, or weakly good-natured, and have a friend who preys on him, and for whom he is disposed to become security. Finally, the beloved Charles, Henry, or Reginald may have none of these propensities, but may chance to be an honest merchant, or a tradesman, with his floating capital in business, and a consequent risk of being one day rich, the next a pauper.

Upon every account, therefore, it is necessary for a young lady to have a settlement on her; and she should not, from a weak spirit of romance, oppose her friends who advise it, since it is for her husband's advantage as well as her own. By making a settlement, there is always a fund that cannot be touched—a something, however small, as a provision for a wife and children; and whether she have a fortune or not, this ought to be made. An allowance for dress should also be arranged; and this should be administered in such a way that a wife should not have to ask for it at inconvenient times, and thus irritate her husband.

Flirtations on either side should be avoided, not only as a matter of etiquette, but of humanity. No one who is really sincere in his professions will wish to inflict pain on the object of his affections. The same remark applies to the other side. Can it be anything but painful in the extreme for a really loving heart to see in the beloved one a tendency to trifle with the most sacred emotions of the heart?

It is not etiquette to make signal displays of devotion in public, or to be constantly sitting apart from the rest of the company; but, on the other hand, "the authorities" will do well to make occasions when the engaged pair can be by themselves, doing so, not ostentatiously, but rather doing it, without speaking of it or drawing attention to it. Nothing can make an engaged couple look more foolish, and feel more uncomfortable, than for the family to quit the room in which all have been sitting, with some such remark as: "Come away! Fanny and Mr. Amor want this room to themselves." Poor Fanny!

In equally bad taste is exclusiveness by the happy couple themselves. Their devotions should be reserved for a *tête-à-tête*, and women are generally in fault when it is otherwise. They like to exhibit their conquest; they cannot dispense with attentions; they forget that the demonstration of any peculiar condition of things in society must make some one uncomfortable: the young ladies are uncomfortable because they are not equally happy; the young gentlemen detest what they call nonsense; the old think there is a time for all things.

All sitting apart, therefore, and especial displays are in bad taste; and they so often accompany insincerity, that the truest affections are apt to be those which are reserved for the genuine and heartfelt intimacy of private interviews.

At the same time, airs of indifference and avoidance should be equally guarded against; since, however strong and mutual attachment may be, such a line of conduct is apt needlessly to mislead others, and so produce mischief. True feeling, and a lady-like consideration for others—a point in which the present generation essentially fails—are the best guides for steering between the extremes of demonstration, on the one hand, and of frigidity on the other.

It is the lady's exclusive privilege to appoint the wedding-day; and however impatient the lover, he must submit patiently to her decree upon this important point.

When the day is fixed, it is customary for the bridegroom to have ready for the occasion a handsome present, usually a parure of jewels, but governed, of course, by his means and generosity.

In France, this gift is called the *corbeille de mariage*, and the rule there is to make its value ten per cent. of the bride's private fortune. It consists of a handsome basket or box, containing shawls, jewels, lace, furs, gloves, fans, and a purse containing a sum of money in *new* gold pieces. This gift is always placed on exhibition with the rest of the wedding presents.

It is etiquette for wedding presents to be sent always to the *bride*, never to the bridegroom, though they be given by friends of the latter. They may be sent at any time during the week previous to the wedding-day, and it is customary to display them, handsomely arranged before the ceremony.

In sending out invitations to a wedding, there are two cards folded in the invitation in the envelope. The invitation is in the name of the bride's mother—or if she is not living, the relative or friend nearest the bride—and is as follows:

MRS. LEON CHURCH
AT HOME,
Wednesday, October 24th,
FROM 11 TILL 2 O'CLOCK.
No. 74 L—— STREET.

The two cards, one large and one small, are folded in this, which is printed upon handsome note-paper. Upon the large card is engraved:

MR. AND MRS. T. L. BURNS.

On the smaller one:

MISS CAROLINE CHURCH.

If, however, there is no bridal reception on the wedding-day, but the young people "receive" after their return from the bridal tour, the card containing their joint names contains also the date of reception, as:

MR. AND MRS. T. L. BURNS
AT HOME,
Wednesday, November 17th,
FROM 11 TILL 2 O'CLOCK.
No. 614 —— STREET.

Or,

MR. AND MRS. T. L. BURNS
AT HOME,
Wednesdays in November,
FROM 11 TILL 2 O'CLOCK.
No. 614 —— STREET.

The bridal calls are not expected to be returned until the last day of reception.

The bridegroom should give to the first groomsman the control of affairs, and the money for the necessary expenses. He it is who presents the snowy bouquet to the bride, the bridegroom making a similar offering to the bridesmaids. It is the first groomsman who leads the visitors up to the young couple for the words of congratulation. It is he who gives the clergyman his fee, who engages the carriages, and, in short, makes all arrangements. If, as is often the case, the whole bridal party go to the depôt to see the happy pair start for the wedding trip, it is then the first groomsman who secures tickets, checks baggage, and secures pleasant seats for the Benedict and bride. It is his duty, also, to send the notice of the marriage to the newspapers. In England but one groomsman, or "best man," is allowed to a bridal party, though the bridesmaids may number a dozen, but in this country one groomsman is allowed for every bridesmaid.

If the wedding takes place in church, it is customary to reserve the front seats in the body of the church for the relatives of the young couple.

It is the height of rudeness for *any one*, whether clergyman, bridegroom, or any member of the bridal train, to keep the bride waiting. The clergyman should be within the rails, the bridegroom and groomsmen should be in the vestry-room, by the time bride is due at the church. The bridesmaids may receive the bride in the vestibule, or may accompany her to the church.

The bridal party should meet in the vestry-room. Then the bride, leaning on the arm of her father, heads the procession; the bridegroom, with the bride's mother upon his arm, follows; then groomsmen and bridesmaids in couples follow.

At the altar, the bridesgroom receives the bride, and the ceremony begins. The groomsmen stand behind the bridesgroom, the bridesmaids behind the bride. The bride and bridegroom remove the right hand-glove in some churches; in others it is not deemed necessary. The bride stands on the left of the groom.

When the wedding takes place at the house of the bride, it is customary to divide the room, either by folding doors or a curtain, and allow the bridal party to be grouped before their friends see them. If, however, this is not convenient, they enter in the same order as in church. It is somewhat customary of late for the bride and groom to walk arm-in-arm to the altar; but it is against established etiquette; the bride should walk with her father, or, if orphaned, with whoever takes the father's place on the occasion.

Where a ring is used, it is the duty of the first bridesmaid to remove the bride's left-hand glove.

After the ceremony, the parents of the bride speak to her first; then the parents of the bridegroom before other friends.

After the ceremony, the bride and groom go in the same carriage from the church to the house, or from the house to the railway depôt.

If there is a breakfast or supper, the bride does not change her dress until she assumes her travelling dress.

If parties are given to the bride and groom, the groomsmen and bridesmaids must be also invited, and, if they prefer, all may wear the dress worn at the wedding. This is, however, optional.

During the fortnight following a wedding, friends of the family should call upon the mother of the bride.

It is contrary to etiquette to wear mourning to a wedding. Even in the case of a widowed mother to either of the happy pair, it is customary to wear gray, or some neutral tint, upon the wedding day, even if the deepest mourning is resumed afterwards.

The bridal dress and the costume of the bridesmaids are not matters that come so much within the province of etiquette as of the fashions, which vary as the winds. All that etiquette requires is that good taste shall guide the whole of the arrangements. Pure white is the only color worn by the young bride, and the full veil of lace, with wreath of orange flowers, is *de rigueur;* but for a widow, pearl-color or tinted silk, without any veil or wreath, is better. If the bride is a maiden no longer young, it is not in good taste to wear the dress of a youthful bride. White gloves, vests, and ties are demanded for the bridegroom and groomsmen. The bridesmaids may wear colors, but a prettier effect is produced by dresses of pure white, with trimmings only of color. The travelling dress of a bride should be very modest in color and fashion, as it is in extremely bad taste to draw attention to the *bride* when travelling.

It is not etiquette, at a wedding or wedding reception, to congratulate the bride; it is the bridegroom who receives congratulations; the bride, wishes for her future happiness. A gentleman or lady who is acquainted with both bride and groom must speak first to the bride; but if a stranger to either, may first speak to the one with whom he is already acquainted, who will then introduce the other. If a stranger to both bride and groom, the first groomsman must make the introduction.

ETIQUETTE FOR BAPTISMS.

In the baptisms of infants there are certain customs in the world of good society, independent of the religious ceremonies. A few hints will suffice, as each sect has its own peculiar forms known to the members of that church; we do not profess to guide these, but merely the worldly observances.

It is not customary to invite mere acquaintances to be godfather or godmother to an infant; these should be tried friends of long standing, or better still, near relations, to whom the obligations thus imposed will be pleasures and not tasks.

Never invite any friends to be godfather or godmother, who are not of the same church as the child to be baptized.

When you are invited to stand godfather or godmother to an infant, never refuse without grave cause, and then do so immediately, that the parents may have time to make other arrangements.

It is unkind, as well as impolite, to refuse to act in this capacity towards children who, from poverty or other reasons, may occupy an inferior position in society to your own.

It is customary to allow the godmother to select herself the godfather.

It is, however, customary for the maternal grandmother and the paternal grandfather to act as sponsors for the first child; the paternal grandmother and the maternal grandfather as sponsors for the second child. If the grand-parents are not living, the nearest relatives of the same church should be invited.

It is customary for the sponsors to make the babe a present. If it is a little boy, the godfather gives a silver cup, with the full name engraved upon it, and the godmother some pretty piece of silver, jewelry, or dress. If a little girl, it is the godmother who gives the cup, and the godfather the other gift. Where the sponsors are wealthy, it is not unusual to fill the christening-cup with gold pieces. The godmother often adds to her gift the christening robe and cap, both trimmed with white ribbons—for a babe should wear only pure white when presented for baptism.

It is contrary to etiquette to invite young persons to stand as sponsors for an infant.

In the Roman Catholic church, it is customary to baptize an infant as soon as possible. If the child is very delicate, it is customary to send at once for the priest, and have the ceremony performed in the bed-room; but if the babe is healthy and likely to live, it is usually taken to the church for baptism, as young as the physician will permit.

In entering the church, the nurse, carrying the child, goes first; then follow the sponsors, who do not walk arm-in-arm; then the father, and after him the invited guests.

When the ceremony commences, the sponsors stand on each side of the child, the godfather on the right, and the godmother on the left.

The babe should be held lying in the arms of the nurse, its head upon the right arm. The cap should be tied so as to be easily unfastened and removed.

When the priest asks who are the sponsors of the child, it is sufficient for them to incline the head, without speaking.

Baptism is a gratuitous ceremony in the church, but it is customary for the father to present some token to the officiating clergyman, in the name of the babe, or, where parents are wealthy, to make a handsome donation to the poor of the parish, through the clergyman.

In the Protestant churches, it is customary to defer the baptism until the mother of the child can be present.

It is always desirable to have the ceremony performed in the church, if possible; but if there is a necessity for it, such as the illness of the child or the parents, it can take place in the house of the parents, by their special request.

No one should ever offer to act as sponsor for a child. It is the privilege of the parents to make the selection amongst their relatives or friends.

If the ceremony is performed at the house of the parents, a carriage must be sent to the house of the clergyman to convey him to the house of the parents, and wait until after the ceremony, to convey him home again. It is extremely rude to expect a clergyman to provide his own conveyance, or to walk.

Friends invited to a christening usually carry some gift to the babe; gentlemen a gift of silver, and ladies some pretty piece of needlework.

If the ceremony is performed in the house of the parents, or if the guests return there from the church, the only refreshments required by etiquette are cake and wine.

The father of the child usually gives a present of money to the nurse who carries the babe to the church.

It is not etiquette to remain long at a christening; and it is better taste for the infant to be removed to the nursery as soon as the ceremony is over. To keep a weary mother sitting up entertaining guests, or a cross, tired child on exhibition, are either of them in bad taste.

For a guest to show any annoyance if a child cries loudly, or is in any way troublesome, is the height of rudeness. Remarks or even frowns are forbidden entirely, even if the infant screams so as to make the voice of the clergyman entirely inaudible.

Etiquette requires that the babe be praised if it is shown to the guests, even if it is a little monster of pink ugliness. Ladies, especially mothers, will *see* something beautiful, if only its helpless innocence, and gentlemen must behold infantile graces, if they cannot actually behold them. "Mother's darling" must be the great attraction at a christening, if it only improves the occasion by a succession of yells.

ETIQUETTE FOR FUNERALS.

WHEN the saddest of all the ceremonies of this life calls forth the sympathy of friends and relatives, there are many little points the observance of which evinces a delicate consideration for the mourners, and a respect for the melancholy occasion.

In entering the house of mourning, a gentleman must remove his hat in the hall, and not replace it while in the house.

Loud talking in the chamber of death is a rudeness which shows not only a want of respect for the dead, but a want of consideration for the grief of the survivors.

All quarrels must be forgotten in the presence of death. Enemies who meet at a funeral are bound by etiquette, if not by feeling, to salute each other with quiet gravity.

Whilst the body of the dead remains in the house, no visitor must expect to see the members of the bereaved family, and no offence may be taken if admission is refused to the nearest friends.

The formalities necessary upon the death of a member of a family entail upon the survivors many painful interviews, many directions, and often most harrowing discussions. It is, therefore, customary to entrust these details to some relative or friend, who, while near enough to carefully direct the affairs, is yet able to bear the trying details better than the members of the immediate family. It is best to select some one accustomed to the discharge of this duty, and more prudent to name a limit for the expenses.

Where there are no funeral arrangements made in the will, the person taking this charge may ask one interview with the nearest relative, but after that, relieve them of all care in the matter. If there is no friend who can undertake these trying duties, it is then customary to make the undertaker the master of the painful ceremonies.

To surround the funeral ceremonies with great parade and pomp is usually more of a vain and ostentatious display than an act of respect towards the dead ; at the same time, any meanness or parsimony is in bad taste. The expenses should be governed by the position of the deceased, and the means of the survivors.

If invitations are sent out, it is customary to have a number printed, and sent to the friends. The following is the usual form:

"You are respectfully invited to attend the funeral of J. J. C——, on Wednesday, the 24th of May, 18—, at 10 o'clock A.M., from his late residence, No. 174 ——— street. To proceed to Laurel Hill Cemetery."

Or, if the services are not at the house:

"You are respectfully invited to attend the funeral of J. J. C——, from the church of the Incarnation, on Wednesday, the 24th of May, at 10 o'clock A.M. To proceed to Laurel Hill Cemetery."

It is contrary to the rules of etiquette to send these invitations by post.

A list of the persons invited must be given to the person directing the funeral ceremonies, and he will give the undertaker a list of the order in which the guests are to be placed in the carriages, if the funeral leaves the city, or the order of the procession if the guests go to the grave on foot.

If the invitation is given through the newspapers, the words "without further notice" must be added, and the guests will not expect another invitation. The list is then omitted, and no especial order observed in placing the guests in carriages or procession.

Guests invited to a funeral must not present themselves before the hour appointed, when the corpse is generally exposed for the last gaze of the friends. It is customary for the family to pay their last visit to the coffin just before that hour, and all intrusion is against the customs of society.

The corpse usually is exposed in a drawing-room, and the family assemble in another apartment, if the services are to be conducted in church, and the guests go from the house there. If, however, the guests are invited to meet the funeral in church, the coffin is usually placed in front of the chancel, with the lid removed, and friends pass, *from the feet to the head*, up one aisle and down another, after the services are over.

If the guests assemble at the house of the deceased, it is customary for some near relative, not of the immediate family, to receive them, and do the honors of the occasion.

The ladies of the family are never expected to see the guests at a funeral; but it is optional with the gentlemen. Strict etiquette at the present day denies the ladies of the family the privilege of following the corpse from the house; but it is a custom "more honored in the breach than in the observance."

When the funeral procession is ready to start, the clergyman leaves the house first, and enters a carriage, which precedes the hearse. Then follows the coffin, which is placed in the hearse; the next carriage is for the immediate family and relatives. Guests stand uncovered while these mourners pass them, no salutation being expected.

The gentleman who does the honors should precede the family as they pass from their room to the carriages, assist them in, close the door, and motion the driver to move slowly forward, and to the next carriage to drive up to the door.

The same order is observed at the church door, where the master of ceremonies assists the mourners to leave and re-enter the carriages.

When the private carriage of the deceased follows the hearse, it should be empty, and precede the other carriages.

If the friends go on foot, and the weather is cold, the gentlemen may wear their hats; but if the weather is mild, it is customary to walk uncovered, with the hat in the right hand.

If the hat is worn, it must be removed as the coffin passes from the hearse to the church, when the guests form a double line, down which it is carried, and the same line and observance must be made after the service, as the coffin is carried from the church to the hearse again.

If lady friends attend a funeral, if they are not in mourning, they should wear grave, quiet colors. To go to a funeral in a gay dress is insulting.

Upon the coffin of an infant or young person, it is customary to place a wreath of white flowers.

Upon the coffin of a married person, a cross of white flowers is usually placed.

Upon the coffin of an army or navy officer, the hat, epaulets, sword, and sash are placed, and it is customary to use the flag to cover the coffin.

A sufficient number of carriages should be provided to carry all invited guests to the cemetery.

At the cemetery, the priest or clergyman walks in advance of the coffin, and the others alight from the carriages and stand around the grave.

After the carriages leave the cemetery, it is not customary for the guests to return to the house of the mourners; but each may, on re-entering the carriage, direct the driver, in a low tone, where to drive him.

The family physician, if able to attend the funeral, should have a seat in the carriage following that of the immediate family.

The carriage must be sent for the priest or clergyman in time for him to be punctually at the house at the appointed hour.

If gifts of flowers are sent to the mourners, they must be white only, and sent on the day of the funeral early enough to be used in the decoration of the coffin.

If pall-bearers are invited, they must be immediate friends of the deceased.

It is a foreign custom of much beauty and significance to select young children for pall-bearers for infants and children, dressing them in white, and draping the coffin in white, trimmed with silver fringe and cords.

If gloves and crape bands are distributed to the gentlemen guests, they must be handed them when they first enter the house. It is a gross violation of etiquette to make any selection in such cases; nobody expects to have gloves so given as to fit the hands; but they must be worn. It is far more elegant to present yourself already provided with black kid gloves on your hands, and allow the undertaker to provide you only with the crape.

Friends in deep mourning are not expected to pay visits of condolence, and are excused from accepting funeral invitations; but all others are expected to accept them. It is but a poor compliment to your friends to attend their dinners, receptions, balls, and parties, and refuse to be present when they are in affliction, or to pay the last act of respect to the memory of those they love.

During the week following a funeral, friends should leave their cards for the family of the deceased, and call again about a fortnight later, asking then to see the members of the family.

It is not customary to ask to see the family of a deceased friend before the funeral; but cards should be sent, and offers of service sent by note.

The lady friend nearest the family, or a relative not of the immediate family, is the proper person to purchase the mourning for the ladies of the family, and the gentleman friend or relative that for the gentlemen.

No member of the immediate family of the deceased should leave the house between the death and the funeral upon any errand or pretext.

At the funeral of a mounted officer, his horse, fully equipped, and draped in mourning, should be led by a servant after the hearse.

If the deceased belonged to any society, as Free Masons, Odd Fellows, or such organization, the society should be invited through a note sent to the President, and they will send word to the master of ceremonies if there is any especial order in which they wish to follow the corpse, or any form or ceremony peculiar to that order which they would like observed. These invitations, if given through the newspapers, should carefully specify the lodge or order to which the deceased belonged. The regalia in such cases is usually displayed on the coffin-lid, but removed before the coffin leaves the house.

White plumes are customary on the hearse of a young person, and black ones for married and elderly people.

It is not customary to send invitations to the funeral of a person who has died of contagious disease, and the statement of the malady in the newspapers is generally accepted by the friends as an excuse for the omission of invitations.

In visiting a cemetery, it is an act of rudeness to stand near a lot where mourners are assembled, or in any way to notice those who are decorating the graves of friends. No time can be named when the delicate attentions and observances of etiquette are more grateful than when sorrow is heavy on the heart.

ETIQUETTE OF THE STUDIO.

There are a few rules of etiquette applicable to visitors to artists' studios, which it will be well to note, the more so because they are special, and might not suggest themselves, as a matter of course, even to those to whom Nature presented the whole code of etiquette when she gave them a gentle disposition.

It is not etiquette to ask an artist the price of his pictures at sight.

If a visitor sees a painting or a piece of statuary which he wishes to possess, he asks simply that he may have the refusal of it; or he says to the artist: "I wish to have this picture, if it is not disposed of." After leaving the studio, the visitor writes and asks the price, of which he is informed by the artist, in writing. Should the price be larger than the would-be purchaser is disposed to give, he writes again to that effect, and it is no breach of etiquette to name the sum which he wished to spend upon the work of art. This gives an opportunity to the artist of lowering his price.

It is not customary, however, to haggle about the sum, and the correspondence should not be carried farther than above, except it be an intimation from the artist that he will accept the terms of the purchaser, and that the picture is subject to his order, and will be sent to him on further instructions.

Some portrait painters have a practice which, for obvious reasons, cannot be adopted by painters of general subjects. They have a card hung up in a conspicuous part of the studio, showing the price at which they will execute portraits of the sizes given. At the bottom of this card there is generally an intimation that half the price must be paid after the first sitting, the remainder when the portrait is completed.

This practice saves time and trouble, and it would be well if other artists could adopt some system whereby the price of such paintings as they may have for sale might be made known to visitors. But the price of a fancy picture is to be ascertained by the artist only by what it will bring, and it is quite likely that the wealth of the buyer, or his known admiration for good paintings, may reasonably make a difference in the sum asked by the artist, who might ask a lower price of a man whom he knew could not afford so much. There is nothing wrong in this, for an artist has as much right to get as much more than the minimum price of his picture as anybody else has to get the best price for his labor or his merchandise.

Portrait painting is, however, pretty much a repetition of the same sort of work, and the artist would be the last man in the world to admit that there could be such difference in the execution of the work as to warrant a scale of prices in conformity therewith.

It is not etiquette to visit the studio of an artist excepting by special invitation, and then only at the hours he may appoint. To go at any other time is ill-bred ; for although he may be there, he will probably be unwilling to be disturbed at his work.

It is ill-bred to take a young child to visit the studio of an artist, as there are generally articles there of value and easily broken or soiled; and even if the child is well trained, the owner of such articles would be in terror lest they should be ruined.

It is excessively ill-bred to criticize harshly, in the presence of an artist, the works displayed in his studio. Extravagant praise is also in bad taste. A few cordial words of praise and pleasure should, of course, be spoken, and a friend may sometimes point out where improvements could be made; but it is a thankless task generally, and it is in much better taste to leave all criticism to the public journals, when the paintings are on public exhibition.

It is against the rules of etiquette to keep an artist waiting, if you are sitting for a portrait. His time is of value to him, whatever yours may be to you; and it is equally rude to detain him after the sitting is over. His politeness may hinder him from even hinting to you that you are trespassing upon his hours for work, though he may be fretting silently at your rudeness in so doing.

It is contrary to the rules of etiquette to look around a studio in which you may be sitting for a portrait, unless you are invited by an artist to do so.

It is against the rules of etiquette to ask to see an unfinished picture, even if it is one that is being painted by your own order.

To uncover any picture or article in a studio that may be veiled or hidden from view is extremely rude. It is equally so to turn a picture that is hung to face the wall, or standing facing it.

Gentlemen must never smoke in a studio, unless especially invited by the artist to do so.

To whisper in a studio is excessively ill-bred; for although you may make a remark entirely independent of what is around you, you may rest assured you will have the credit of having ridiculed or censured some of the pictures you have been invited to examine.

To behave in a studio as if you were in a store, pricing pictures, inquiring about what is for public exhibition, what is not; who ordered this picture or that; whose portrait this or that may be; or in any way reminding the artist that his genius is merchandise, is rude and indelicate.

It is against the rules of etiquette to handle the pictures or other articles in a studio.

It is extremely rude, if an artist continues his employment during a visit to his studio, for the visitor to stand behind him, or very near him, or in any way to seem to watch his work.

TABLE ETIQUETTE.

It is impossible for a lady or gentleman to act with perfect ease and graceful manner at table when in company, at a hotel or any public place, unless they habitually pay attention to those minor points of etiquette, which form so distinctive a mark of perfectly good breeding. Habitual neglect of the courtesies and etiquette of the table will make them appear awkward restraints upon occasions when they are important. If the father or mother of a family accustom the children, by example as well as precept, to be attentive and polite to each other at every meal, they need never fear that they will shame them by rudeness or awkwardness when they go abroad.

Even when a person habitually eats alone, it is better to do so gracefully and with attention to the rules of etiquette, that habits of awkwardness may not be formed, which it will be difficult to shake off when in company.

To make noises when eating, sucking soup with a gurgling sound, chewing meat noisily, swallowing as if with an effort, smacking the lips, or breathing heavily while masticating food, are all marks of low breeding.

It is a bad habit to put large pieces of food into the mouth. If you are addressed suddenly with your mouth so filled, you are obliged to make an awkward pause before answering, or to run the risk of choking by swallowing the great mouthful too hastily.

Never open the napkin entirely, but let it lie on the lap, partly folded.

Sit neither very near nor very far from the table.

It is rude to move your arms at table so as to incommode those on either side of you.

Ladies should, after seating themselves, endeavor to draw their skirts into a space that will not crowd those seated beside them.

To lean back in the chair is rude, and surely no gentleman would ever be guilty of tipping his chair at table. Sit erect, not stiffly, but in an easy position.

Bread must always be broken, never cut, and certainly never bitten.

If a plate is sent to you filled with the food you have selected, keep it, as others may not have the same choice; if the plate contain one dish, such as pie or pudding, you may pass it on to those beside you, and wait till others above you are served before reserving a plate for yourself.

To eat very fast is inelegant; to eat very slowly bears an air of affectation. Try to preserve the happy medium.

It is a good plan to accustom yourself to eat with the left hand, and thus avoid shifting your knife and fork from one hand to the other.

A gentleman will always see that ladies are served before eating himself.

Avoid making any noise on your plate with your knife and fork.

It is against all rules of etiquette to soak up gravy with bread, to scrape up sauce with a spoon, or to take up bones with the fingers.

Never cross the knife and fork on a plate until you have finished eating.

Never hold your knife and fork erect in your hands at each side of your plate, when conversing at the table.

Never ask for a second helping. It is the duty of those at the head and foot of the table to offer it.

To blow soup to cool it, or to pour tea or coffee into a saucer for the same purpose, are acts of awkwardness never seen in polite society. Wait until they are cool enough to be pleasant.

Use the salt-spoon, butter-knife, and sugar-tongs even when you are alone.

If you want to cough, sneeze, or blow your nose, leave the table. If you have not time, turn away your head, and lean back in your chair.

To pass a plate with a knife or fork upon it, or a cup with a spoon in it, are acts of rudeness. Put your spoon in the saucer, and your knife and fork on the table, until you are served.

Never hurry away from the table as soon as you finish eating, if others remain to converse. If you are obliged to leave before a meal is finished or immediately after, ask to be excused for so doing, and apologize for the necessity.

Never mention at the table any subject that is likely to disgust others. It is a piece of rudeness only too common, and is to be severely censured. Many who are utterly without affectation are really sensitive on such points, and their meal and comfort are both spoiled if disgusting associations are suggested at table.

At home, if you use a napkin-ring, fold your napkin and replace it in the ring when you have done with it. If you are dining out, never fold your napkin, but place it beside your plate.

None but a clown would use the table-cloth for a napkin, pick his teeth with his fork, put his fingers in his plate, or wipe his face with his napkin.

If you are unfortunate enough to find anything disgusting in your food—a hair in the soup, a coal in the bread, a worm in the fruit, or a fly in your coffee—do not loudly exclaim, or disturb the appetite of others by mention of your mishap. Remove the disgusting object quietly, or change your cup or plate without remark.

The French poet, Delille, tells of an interview between himself and Marmoutel, which rather humorously points out how table etiquette may change.

Delille and Marmoutel were dining together, in the month of April, 1786, and the conversation happened to turn upon dinner-table customs. Marmoutel observed how many little things a well-bred man was obliged to know, if he would avoid being ridiculous at the table of his friends.

"They are, indeed, innumerable," said Delille, "and the most annoying fact of all is, that not all the wit and good sense in the world can help one to divine them untaught. A little while ago, for instance, the Abbé Cosson, who is Professor of Literature at Collége Mazarin, was describing to me a grand dinner to which he had been invited at Versailles, and to which he had sat down in the company of peers, princes, and marshals of France.

"'I'll wager now,' said I, 'that you committed a hundred blunders in the etiquette of the table.'

"'How so?' replied the Abbé, somewhat nettled. 'What blunders could I make? It seems to me that I did precisely as others did.'

"'And I, on the contrary, would stake my life that you did nothing as others did. But let us begin at the beginning, and see which is right. In the first place, there was your table napkin—what did you do with that when you sat down to table?'

"'What did I do with my table napkin? Why, I did like the rest of the guests: I shook it out of the folds, spread it before me, and fastened one corner to my button-hole.'

"'Very well, *mon cher*, you were the only person who did so. No one shakes, spreads, and fastens a table napkin in that manner. You should have only laid it across your knees. What soup had you?'

"'Turtle.'

"'And how did you eat it?'

"'Like every one else, I suppose. I took my spoon in one hand and my fork in the other.'

"'Your fork? Good heavens! None but a savage eats soup with a fork. But go on. What did you take next?'

"'A boiled egg.'

"'Good. And what did you do with the shell?'

"'Not eat it, certainly. I left it, of course, in the egg-cup.'

"'Without breaking it through with your spoon?'

"'Without breaking it.'

"'Then, my dear fellow, permit me to tell you that no one eats an egg without breaking the shell, and leaving the spoon standing in it. And after your egg?'

"'I asked for some *bouilli*.'

"'For *bouilli!*' It is a term that no one uses. You should have asked for beef; never for *bouilli.* Well, and after the *bouilli?*'

"'I asked the Abbé de Badenvillais for some fowl.'

"'Wretched man! Fowl indeed! You should have asked for chicken or capon. The word "fowl" is never heard out of the kitchen. But all this applies only to what you ate; tell me something of what you drank, and how you asked for it.'

"'I asked for Champagne and Bordeaux from those who had the bottles before them.'

"'Know, then, my good friend, that only a waiter, who has no time or breath to spare, asks for Champagne or Bordeaux. A gentleman asks for Vin de Champagne and Vin de Bordeaux. But now inform me how you ate your bread.'

"'Undoubtedly like all the rest of the world: I cut it up into small square pieces with my knife.'

"'Then let me tell you that no one cuts bread; you should always break it. Let us go on to the coffee. How did you drink yours?'

"'Pshaw! At least, I could make no mistake in that. It was boiling hot; so I poured it, a little at a time, in the saucer, and drank it as it cooled.'

"'*Eh bien!* Then you assuredly acted as no other gentleman in the room. Nothing can be more vulgar than to pour tea or coffee into a saucer. You should have waited till it cooled, and then have drunk it from the cup. And now you see, my dear cousin, that so far from doing precisely as the others did, you acted in no one respect according to the laws prescribed by etiquette.'"

ETIQUETTE WITH CHILDREN.

It is against the rules of strict etiquette to take a child when making formal calls, as they are a restraint upon conversation, even if they are not troublesome about touching forbidden articles, or teasing to go home.

Never take a child to a funeral, either to the house of mourning or to the cemetery.

Never allow a child to take a meal at a friend's house without special invitation. It is impossible to know how much she may be inconvenienced, while her regard for the mother would deter her from sending the little visitor home again.

Never allow a child to handle goods in a store.

Never send for children to meet visitors in the drawing-room, unless the visitors themselves request to see them. Make their stay then very brief, and be careful that they are not troublesome.

Never take a child to church until it is old enough to remain perfectly quiet. Although you may be accustomed to its restless movements, and not disturbed by them, others near you will certainly feel annoyed by them.

It is not etiquette to put a child to sleep in the room of a guest, nor to allow children to go at all to a guest's room, unless especially invited to do so, and even then to make long stay there.

Etiquette excludes children from all companies given to grown persons, from all parties and balls, excepting such as are given especially given for their pleasure.

When invited to walk or drive, never take a child, unless it has been invited, or you have requested permission to do so; even in the latter case, the consent is probably given more from good-nature than from any desire to have a juvenile third to the party.

Never crowd children into pic-nic parties, if they have not been invited. They generally grow weary and very troublesome before the day is over.

Never take a child to spend the day with a friend unless it has been included in the invitation.

Never allow children to be in the drawing-room if strangers are present.

Never allow children to handle the ornaments in the drawing-room of a friend.

Never allow a child to pull a visitor's dress, play with the jewelry or ornaments she may wear, take her parasol or satchel for a plaything, or in any way annoy her.

Train children early to answer politely when addressed, to avoid restless, noisy motions when in company, and gradually inculcate a love of the gentle courtesies of life. By making the rules of etiquette habitual to them, you remove all awkwardness and restraint from their manners when they are old enough to go into society.

Never send a child to sit upon a sofa with grown people, unless they express a desire to have it do so.

Never crowd a child into a carriage seat between two grown people.

Never allow a child to play with a visitor's hat or cane.

If children are talented, be careful you do not weary your friends, and destroy their own modesty by "showing them off," upon improper occasions. What may seem wonderful to an interested mother, may be an unuttterable weariness to a guest, too polite to allow the mother to perceive the incipient yawn.

Never allow children to visit upon the invitation of other children. When they are invited by the older members of the family, it is time to put on their "best bibs and tuckers."

Never take children to a house of mourning, even if you are an intimate friend.

The custom for having children in the drawing-room for morning or evening parties, or in the dining-room with the dessert at dinner companies, is not only often an annoyance to the guests, but bad for the children themselves.

It is one of the first duties of parents to train their children at home as they would have them appear abroad. An English lady writes thus :

"If, then, we desire that our children shall become ladies and gentlemen, can we make them so, think you, by lavishing money upon foreign professors, dancing-masters, foreign travel, tailors, and dressmakers? Ah, no! good breeding is far less costly, and begins far earlier than those things. Let our little ones be nurtured in an atmosphere of gentleness and kindness from the nursery upwards; let them grow up in a home where a rude gesture or an ill-tempered word are alike unknown; where between father and mother, master and servant, mistress and maid, friend and friend, parent and child, brother and sister, prevails the law of truth, of kindness, of consideration for others, and forgetfulness of self. Can they carry into the world, whither we send them later, aught of coarseness, of untruthfulness, of slatternliness, of vulgarity, if their home has been orderly, if their parents have been refined, their servants well mannered, their friends and playmates kindly and carefully trained as themselves? Do we want our boys to succeed in the world; our girls to be admired and loved; their tastes to be elegant; their language choice; their manners simple, charming, refined, and graceful; their friendship elevating? then we must ourselves be what we would have our children to be, remembering the golden maxim, that good manners, like charity, must begin at home.

"Good manners are an immense social force. We should, therefore, spare no pains to teach our children what to do, and what to avoid doing, in their pathway through life.

"On utilitarian as well as social principles, we should try to instruct our children in good manners; for whether we wish them to succeed in the world, or to adorn society, the point is equally important. We must never lose sight of the fact, that here teachers and professors can do little, and that the only way in which it in possible to acquire the habits of good society is, to live in no other."

GAMES WITH CARDS.

Married ladies and elderly gentlemen are allowed to claim precedence at the card-table, over single young ladies and the younger men. Ladies of "a certain age," if single, can claim the privileges of the card-table with married ladies.

Etiquette does not require any one to play unwillingly. It is very rude to urge the request, as many have conscientious scruples on this matter, though they may not care to wound the feelings of those playing by proclaiming them.

It is not kind, however, and therefore it is not etiquette, to refuse to play, if there are no such scruples, when the refusal prevents a game being made up.

None should attempt to play—whist, for instance—unless really able to do so moderately well. It is not fair to impose a poor part ner upon one who may be really fond of the game and play well.

It is not etiquette for those very fond of card-playing to victimize every guest by producing cards whenever they call; whether they care for playing or not. Many will play from good-nature who would prefer to pass the time in conversation.

Husband and wife, or any partners who may be supposed to be intimately acquainted with each other's play, should not play together. It is taking an unfair advantage of the other couple for them to play partners.

If playing for stakes, the gentleman pays for his lady partner in the event of loss; but does not receive her winnings.

All violations of the known rules of the game are violations of the laws of etiquette as well. Yet, if such violations are made, they should be pointed out in a quiet and courteous manner, not made the subject of violent dispute or censure. Any altercations are violations of the laws of etiquette. Loss of temper, no matter how continuous the ill-luck, is a breach of manners; so are objurgations of one's partner's performances, and criticisms on the play of partner or adversary. In whist, as in marriage, the partner is taken for better for worse, and in neither case should an ill-assorted couple try to make matters worse than they are by grumbling and growling at each other.

It is a breach of etiquette to talk constantly upon other subjects whilst engaged in a game of cards. Whist, as all good players know, is a game that requires close attention, and almost absolute silence; and the other games can be much disturbed by talking.

To converse with those who are not playing is still worse. It is a violation of all courtesy to allow the attention to be diverted at all. If addressed while at the game, make your answer as brief as politeness will permit, and give your whole attention to the game again. No one can play so well with divided attention; and you may be certain it is an annoyance to your partner, even if your opponent does not object to it.

Any appearance of an understanding between partners, as

smiles, nods, or winks, are gross violations, not only of the laws of the game, but of good manners.

To finger the cards whilst they are being dealt, is a breach of good manners. Even if you do not violate the laws of the game by actually looking at them, you are committing an error in etiquette by seeming to be in any way aware of their existence before you are at liberty to take them in your hand.

Never start a conversation that would lead to long argument or discussion in the pauses of the game. Small talk, chit-chat, is certainly admissible whilst the cards are being dealt, but only upon topics which can be readily dropped when the play is again the leading subject.

To play cards with an air of weariness or abstraction is positively rude. If you are not interested in the game, strive to appear so, and if you are not equal to that, you had better stop playing.

Try to avoid argument upon nice points in playing. Even if you are right, it is more courteous to yield to your adversary than to keep others waiting whilst you prove your position.

Etiquette by no means requires stakes of money. If counters are not provided for betting games, you may refuse to bet, without any breach of good manners.

In your own house, never offer guests any but *new* cards to play with.

It is a violation of etiquette to propose card-playing in another person's house. This is the privilege of the host or hostess, and if they do not suggest the amusement, it is absolutely rude for any one else to do so.

It is a breach of etiquette to hurry others who are playing. Nothing annoys a deliberate player more than to have a partner or adversary constantly saying, "Come, play; it is your turn now," or, "We are all waiting for you."

Even if you take no pleasure in cards, some knowledge of the etiquette and rules belonging to the games most in vogue will be useful to you, unless you object upon principle to playing. If so, it is better at once to state the fact. If not, and a fourth hand is wanted at a rubber, or if the rest of the company sit down to a round game, you will be deemed guilty of a want of politeness if you refuse to join.

The games most common are whist, loo, euchre, vingt-un, and speculation.

Whist requires four players. A pack of cards being spread upon the table, with their faces downward, the four players draw for partners. Those who draw the two highest, and those who draw the two lowest, become partners. The lowest of all claims the deal.

In declaring that married people may not play at the same table, society by no means understands anything so disgraceful as dishonest collusion; but persons who play regularly together cannot fail to know so much of each other's mode of acting under given circumstances that the chances no longer remain perfectly even in favor of their adversaries.

VISITING CARDS.

The fashion of cards is a variable one. It may be the fashion to-day to have them large, square, and printed upon rough surfaces; to-morrow they may be small, long, and highly glazed; now they are engraved; now written. In fact, there are too many freaks and changes to mention all; but etiquette requires always perfect simplicity. An ornamental visiting card is simply detestable.

Glazed cards are not now in vogue, but they may be again, and ladies' cards are cut much smaller than those used by gentlemen.

Persons who have a city and country residence must have two sets of cards, with the residence at the time of calling engraved on the left-hand corner, thus

MRS. JOHN POTTS,

No. 27 ——— Street,

while Mrs. Potts is in the city, and

MRS. JOHN POTTS,

Cedars,

when Mrs. Potts is out of town.

Visiting cards must never bear a business address.

All merely honorary or official designations must be omitted, except in cards designed for official visits only.

Officers of the army or navy may use their title or not, as preferred, as:

CAPT. JAMES BURNS,
U. S. A.,

Or,

JAMES BURNS,
U. S. A.,

are either of them correct, the former having the advantage of putting the receiver in possession at once of his visitor's rank, the latter allowing scope for promotion or change of title. For militia officers to use their titles upon visiting cards is a piece of affectation utterly absurd. Members of Congress are always entitled to use the "Hon." before the name on their visiting cards, even after their term of office has expired. Judges and physicians are also allowed to use their titles; but no other professional men.

Cards should be engraved in simple Italian characters, and without flourish, embossed surface, or even ostentatiously large letters.

Every visiting card should have the address in small letters in the left-hand corner. If used when in a strange city, the usual address may be scored in lead-pencil, and the temporary one written under the name, thus:

MR. AND MRS. WILLIAM LEIGH,
~~No. 207 ——— Street.~~ St. James Hotel.

It is optional with unmarried ladies to use the prefix to their names.

Gentlemen without military, naval, official, or professional titles generally omit any prefix. but may use the abbreviation "Mr." if they desire.

Autograph visiting cards are conceited affectations. The autograph of distinguished characters may be desirable; but it is precisely that class of people who would be least likely to use them. A neatly engraved card is *en règle;* printed ones look cheap, and are not suitable for visiting.

Persons in mourning should use cards with black borders.

Young unmarried ladies may use separate cards, or may have their names added to their mother's, thus:

MRS. JOSEPH BANKS.
MISS LUCY BANKS.

Leave-taking cards have P. P. C. (*pour prendre congé*) written in the right-hand corner.

Wedding cards are in the best taste when perfectly simple.

It is a breach of etiquette to leave a card after being informed that the person visited is at home.

When you have been informed of an important event in the family of a friend—a birth, a marriage, or a death—if you are unable to offer personal congratulation or condolence, you may leave a card within a week.

If you reside in another city, you may send your card by post, with the word "felicitation" under the name. A mournful event calls for a letter.

A card left for two or more members of the same family must have a corner turned down.

A card with a photograph portrait upon it, though to a certain extent fashionable, is a vulgarism that can never obtain general favor. If you are a gentleman, your visage may be reserved by the chambermaid, to exhibit as "one of her beaux," and no lady, surely, would ever display her face on a visiting card.

Gentlemen presenting flowers or other gifts to ladies should always attach a card, and over the name write, "With compliments of ———."

Christmas gifts, when sent, should be accompanied by the card of the giver.

Loans of books or music, when returned, should always be accompanied by the card of the borrower.

LETTER WRITING.

No one should write letters at all who cannot write in a clear, fair hand, that "those who run may read." In a busy age like the present, when every one's time has a certain value, we have no right to impose the reading of hieroglyphics upon our correspondents. "I's" should be dotted, "t's" crossed, and capitals used in their proper places, and only the most obvious abbreviations indulged in. Punctuation is equally *de regueur*; the most unimportant letters should be carefully punctuated; and the habit is so easily acquired, and so simple, that after a while it entails no more time or thought than dotting the "i's."

The handwriting of a lady or gentleman should not be commercial or scholastic, but firm and characteristic. All affectations in writing should be avoided, such as sloping one's hand to the left, the use of flourishes, undue size in the characters, or a diminutiveness of the same to try eyesight and patience. The signature should be simple and unostentatious. Nothing can be more absurd than to see a person whose name can have no significance to the world in general, sign himself as elaborately as if he were the Pope or President at least.

Underlining should only be resorted to when the underlined word is of really great importance. Many ladies carry this practice to excess, and so rob it of all significance, as a speaker who emphasized every other word would not be heeded when he needed to be emphatic. What can be more absurd than such a sentence as the following:

"We are *all* very *sorry* to hear that you *cannot* come to *visit* us this *summer*, as we *expected*, and wish your *business* was not so *engrossing*."

For the ordinary correspondence of a lady or gentleman it is advisable to use white note-paper of good quality, and the size distinguished as "commercial note."

If monograms or initials are used, they should be as simple as possible, and in white or black only. Gilt or colored monograms are in bad taste.

Red sealing-wax is admissible only for business letters, and wafers are entirely out of style.

In mourning, the paper and envelopes may have a black border suitable to the relationship of the dead, and the length of time the mourning has been worn. In the deepest mourning, exaggerations of black border are unbecoming and in bad taste. Real grief is always unostentatious.

No letter should contain erasures under any circumstances.

The stamp should be placed exactly in the right-hand corner of the envelope; it must neither be up-side-down, nor slanting, nor in any way carelessly affixed. Negligence in these matters evinces a rudeness to the person to whom you write, as hinting that you think anything will do.

Blots and smears are almost too gross pieces of carelessness to be commented upon. After ten years of age, they are entirely inexcusable.

Never omit your own name and address from a letter, whether of business or friendship.

In writing to persons with whom you are but slightly acquainted, use as few words as possible. You are not authorized in taking up much of their time. It is only in correspondence with very intimate friends that long letters are permissible. If occasion necessitates a letter to a very busy person, politeness requires that it should be framed as curtly as is consistent with civility and perspicuity. It is unpardonable to waste really valuable time, because we do not choose to be at the trouble of concentrating our thoughts and sparing our words.

In writing to our friends or acquaintances, we should never communicate bad news abruptly; but should lead the way to it in such a manner as to soften the blow. A great deal of pain may be avoided by a proper choice of words.

We should scrupulously avoid writing too frequently, or at too great a length, of our own losses and misfortunes. To do this is merely thoughtless egotism. We may have a right to expect sympathy from our friends, but we have no right to make our letters inflictions. Letters should invariably be written cheerfully if possible, and, at least, in a tone of resignation.

An ill-tempered letter is as great a mistake as a lachrymose one. Nothing is so inexpedient as to write a letter in a fit of indignation and anger. If you must give way to your feelings, write your letter, but let it remain unposted until the next day; read it over then, and you will probably put it in the fire.

It is better, if possible, to seek an interview with the person who has wronged or affronted you. Spoken recrimination or reproof is forgotten; but when you have once written down and issued your angry thoughts, they are irrevocable, and a sure source of after regret.

In dealing with those who may have treated you unfairly, be civil in your letters. Be as haughty as you please, and state your grievance in plain, unvarnished terms, and there end. If the truth does not sting, nothing you can add to it will do so; and vituperation, though it does not injure the person upon whom you bestow it, injures your own cause, and detracts seriously from the proper dignity of your own position.

In writing, as in conversation, egotism is a capital offence. We have no more right to be egotistic on paper than we have a right to be dull or disagreeable. A letter should be like a visit, bright, inspiriting, and a reflex of our best mood. Above all, it should be kind and sympathetic.

There are letters whose arrival we hail as we should that of a new book by a delightful writer, or the visit of a brilliant acquaintance.

Again, there are others, the delivery of which, anticipating all the dullness and verbosity with which they are certain to be filled, we dread like the incursions of a well-known bore. Who would not wish to be the writer of the one? Who would not take any amount of pains with his correspondence to avoid being dreaded as the other?

Always answer any letter that may be addressed to you, no matter who the writer may be. If the letter be from one who has no business to write to you, nevertheless acknowledge it, and by your style and manner check further impertinence. Thus:

WASHINGTON, D. C., Jan. 7th, 18—.

SIR:

I write to acknowledge the receipt of your letter of the 5th inst., acquainting me with your opinion of my speech in Congress on the 27th ultimo

I am, sir,

Your obedient servant,

JAMES M. ——.

MR. P. C. LITTLETON,
Philadelphia.

Business letters generally have the name of the firm or person to whom they are addressed written above the "Gentlemen." or "Sir," as:

"Messrs. Dick & Fitzgerald:
"Gentlemen,"

Or,

"John Brown, Esq.:
"Dear sir."

The name of the place from which the letter is written, the date, the full name of writer and receiver, should be given in some part of a letter. The practice of heading a note "Monday," without a date, and signing it "Charlie," is very embarrassing; it makes it difficult to answer a note unless immediately, when the day of the week can be readily identified with the day of the month, and when the receiver knows who his correspondent really is. Besides this, in the event of the letter miscarrying, it cannot be returned if there be no surname attached to the signature. A most important lawsuit in London was lost by a letter, of great value and significance otherwise, being dropped from the evidence for want of identification, being directed, "Dearest Tootings," and signed, "Your loving Poppets." It may seem absurd that a letter of weight could contain such silliness; but it was a fact.

Do not write on scraps of paper, as if your correspondence were not worth the cost of a proper sheet. Neither use old envelopes turned, as some people are wont to do.

Always be sure that your letter has sufficient stamps upon it to fully prepay its weight.

Do not enclose stamps for an answer unless the matter be a business one, and your own proper affair.

Should you send manuscript subject to approval to an editor, enclose stamps sufficient to pay for its return. You have no right to put another to this expense, especially as you already require from him a sacrifice of time, in order to look over what you have sent.

Anonymous communications are both cowardly and ill-bred. Under no circumstances should they be written. The fire is the only fit asylum for them when received. The Gunpowder Plot might have been revealed open-handedly, and the anonymous letter even in that case nearly missed its aim. The only anonymous communications which can be tolerated are the harmless missives called valentines. These, however, have fallen out of favor in polite society. Children and servants are the chief supporters of the manufacturers of the gorgeous love-letters.

In writing to a person who is the guest of another, take care to place the name of the host or hostess on the cover of your letter. Some people address the letter in such a case to the host, and inscribe the name of their correspondent in the left-hand corner, thus :

JAMES GORDON, ESQ.,
No. 347 ——— Street,
New York.

For Mrs. T. C. BATES.

This practice is very likely to lead to an unintentional opening of the letter by the wrong person; for a cursory glance at the cover would seem to show that the letter was intended for the person whose name was most prominent. The letter should have been directed, to the person for whom it was intended first, thus :

Mrs. T. C. BATES,
Care of JAMES GORDON, Esq.,
No. 347 ——— Street,
New York.

Unless very well acquainted with your correspondent, do not use terms implying intimacy.

Business letters usually commence with "Sir," "Gentlemen," "Dear Sir," or "Dear Sirs," and end with, "I am, Sir (or Gentlemen), Your obedient servant," etc.

Official letters invariably begin with the title of the person addressed, and then "Sir," if a civilian or the rank of an officer.

If the letter be to the head of a Department, to a high Government official, or to a superior officer, it is customary to write in a strain a little more deferential than ordinary, so that, instead of saying, as you would to a friend, "I have to acquaint you," "I have to acknowledge the receipt of your letter," you would say, "I have the honor to acknowledge." The ending, too, of such letters should be slightly different: "I have the honor to be, General, Your obedient servant," taking the place of "I am, sir," etc.

In official communications, margins are always left, so as to allow of notations being made for the purpose of framing an answer, and the backs of the pages should be left blank for the same purpose. It is not customary to write down quite to the bottom of the page, but to take ample room for the substance of the letter.

Unless writing officially, or to some public person, it is not customary in this country to give a man all the titles which may belong to him.

Remember that "brevity is the soul of wit." Let your letters be concisely written, not too bluntly, but in a clear, straightforward style, going at once to the subjects you desire to mention, with as little preamble as possible. Use the passive instead of the active voice. To do so prevents the continual thrusting forward of the first person singular into the letter, and gives a more modest appearance to the text.

Short notes to strangers on business—as, for instance, in reference to the character of a servant, asking for some information, etc.—should be written in the third person singular, thus:

"Mrs. Wright presents her compliments to Mrs. Left, and will feel greatly obliged by any information respecting the character and qualifications of Jane Broom, who has applied for a situation as housemaid in Mrs. Wright's household.

"No. 27 F—— Street, Jan 9th, 1869."

The answer should also be written in the third person, and should contain as much information as possible relative to the points inquired about, stating whether the servant is honest, sober, and truthful, and what is her experience of her disposition and habits.

In writing to a servant, or to one considerably below your own station, the following form may be used:

"Jane Broom is hereby informed that Mrs. Wright is willing to engage her as housemaid from the 15th of January, 1869.

"No. 27 F—— Street, Jan. 10th, 1869."

Or this:

"Jane Broom—your character is satisfactory, and you can enter my service on Saturday, the 15th of January."

Or this:

"Mrs. Wright is satisfied with Jane Broom's character, and informs her that she may enter Mrs. Wright's service as housemaid on Saturday next."

In sending any communication to a newspaper or magazine, address to "The Editor," and not to any private person connected with the publication. By so doing, you will better secure attention than if you trouble the editor at his own house by addressing him by his own name. Besides this, some one may be acting for the editor, and if he sees the packet addressed to the name of the absentee, he will not feel free to open it, but will send it to him, whereby confusion and delay, possibly loss of the manuscript, may ensue.

There are six parts to every letter: the date, the complimentary address, the body of the letter, the complimentary closing, the signature, the address or superscription; thus:

(*Date*) PETERSBURG, Va., June 18th, 1869.

(*Complimentary address*) JAMES MUNROE, ESQ.:

DEAR SIR:

(*Body of the letter*) Your most welcome letter, announcing your intention of visiting our city, reached me this morning. I hasten to answer to beg that you will make my house your home during your stay, and inform me by what train I may expect you, that I may meet you at the depot. Leaving all else for the first conversation,

(*Complimentary closing*) I am, my dear friend,

Yours very truly,

(*Signature*) P. T. JONES.

(*Address or Superscription*)
JAMES MONROE, ESQ.,
Bangor, Maine.

THE LADY'S TOILET.

PERHAPS, in these days of public and private baths, it may seem a work of supererogation to insist upon cleanliness as the first requisite in a lady's toilet. Yet it may be as well to remind our fair readers that fastidiousness on this head cannot be carried too far. Cleanliness is the outward sign of inward purity. Cleanliness is health, and health is beauty.

We will begin, then, with the business of the dressing-room, which can be quite well performed in three-quarters of an hour, or even less; and should at latest be achieved by eight o'clock in summer, and nine in winter. To sleep too much is as trying to the constitution as to sleep too little. To sleep too much is to render oneself liable to all kinds of minor ailments, both of mind and body. It is a habit that cannot be too severely censured, especially in the young. No mother has any right to allow her young daughters to ruin their temper, health, and complexion, by lying in bed till nine or ten o'clock. Early rising conduces more to the preservation of health, freshness, and young looks, than anything in the world, and even to the proper preservation of our mental faculties.

The bath is a most important object of study. It is not to be supposed that we wash in order to become clean; we wash because we wish to remain clean. The bath should be taken by a person in good health once a day in winter, and twice a day in summer. For persons of really robust constitutions, a cold shower-bath may be recommended; but as a general rule the sponge-bath is safest and most convenient. Cold water refreshes and invigorates, but does not cleanse; those persons, therefore, who daily use a cold bath in the morning should frequently use a warm one at night. For cleansing purposes, the water should be of from ninety-six to one hundred degrees, or even one hundred and eight degrees; but such a bath should be sparingly indulged in, as it exhausts the physical powers.

A tepid bath, varying from eighty-five to ninety-five degrees, is perhaps the safest for general use, the more particulary as it answers the purpose both of refreshing and cleansing. It is not well to remain in the bath for longer than two or three miuutes. A large coarse sponge is best for the purpose. It is advisable to wet the top of the head before entering a cold bath. Whether soap be used or not, it is well to apply the flesh-brush gently to the face and vigorously to the whole body. Nothing improves the complexion like the daily use of the flesh-brush. When the brushing is concluded, a huck-a-back or Turkish towel should be used for the final process of drying.

The teeth must be scrupulously cared for. If proper care were taken of the teeth in youth, there would be less employment for the dentist in after life. The Americans ruin their teeth by drinking iced drinks with hot dinners; the Spanish ladies by eating sugar all day long; the Mexicans by smoking cigarettes. Very hot and very sweet things should be avoided. The teeth should be carefully brushed, not only night and morning, but after every meal. Very hard tooth-brushes are not advisable, and a simple tooth-powder of common chalk is safer and more effectual than any quackeries. The onion, we need scarcely observe, must be the forbidden fruit of the Eve of the nineteenth century. Indigestible food is also certain to affect the sweetness of the breath. As soon as the breath becomes unpleasant, one may be quite sure that the digestive machinery is out of order.

The nails must always be fastidiously clean, and never allowed to grow inordinately long. In the cutting of the nails, every care must be gvien to the preservation of the shape, and to the removal of superfluous skin. A liberal use of the nail-brush, warm water, and best Windsor soap will insure the preservation of a delicate hand. Gloves must of course be worn out of doors; and even indoors as much as possible.

The hair requires a good deal of care, though of the simplest and most inartificial kind. The secret of fine and glossy hair is a clean hair-brush; and ladies who keep no maid to perform those offices for them should wash their hair-brushes in hot water and soda every day. Every other day is the minimum of washing that a hair-brush should have.

Once secure the perfect cleanliness of your hair-brush, and the rest will be easy. Brush the hair carefully both at night and morning; let it be occasionally cleansed with yolk of egg beaten up, or a mixture of glycerine and lime-juice, and you will find no need to resort to hair-doctors or quacks. Pomade and oil are strictly to be avoided; but after a sea-water bath, or during a sea journey, a little warm pomade will be useful in softening the hair.

Above all things, never attempt to change the color of the hair by means of fashionable dyes and fluids. Color so obtained cannot harmonize naturally with the skin, eyes, and eyebrows that Nature has given. Practices of this kind are simply and strictly immodest. They evince a senseless desire for fashion, and an equally senseless eagerness to attract. Auricomus hair-dyes, like painted lips and cheeks, and pencilled eyebrows, and complexions purchased, are disgraceful to the wearers. With regard to the art of obtaining a good complexion, let ladies be careful in regard to diet, take regular exercise in the open air, wear broad-brimmed hats in the sun, and veils in the wind; let them avoid pearl powders and washes of every kind; let them, above all things, go early to bed, and rise betimes in the morning; and if by so doing they are not made " beautiful forever," they can never be made so.

The face should never be washed when heated from exercise. Wipe the perspiration from the skin, and wait until it is sufficiently cool before you bathe, even with warm water. Rain-water is best for the bath. In case of any eruption upon the skin, no time should be lost in procuring medical advice. He who doctors himself, says the proverb, has a fool for his physician.

With regard to dress, it is impossible to do more than offer a few general observations. The fashion of dress is for to-day; but the æsthetics of dress are for all time. No matter to what absurd lengths fashion may go, a woman of taste will ever avoid the ridiculous. The milliner and dressmaker may handle the scissors never so despotically, but in matters of color, harmony, and contrast they remain under the control of their employer. Dress, indeed, may fairly claim to be considered in the light of a fine art. To dress well demands something more than a full purse and a pretty figure. It requires taste, good sense, and refinement.

A woman of taste and good sense will neither make dress her first nor her last object in life. She will remember that no wife should betray that total indifference for her husband's taste which is implied in the neglect of her appearance; and she will also remember that to dress consistently and tastefully is one of the duties which she owes to society.

There is a Spanish proverb which says, " Every hair has its shadow." So, in like manner, every lady, however insignificant her social position may appear to herself, must exercise a certain influence on the feelings and opinions of others. If, therefore, the art of dressing appears either too irksome or too frivolous to such of the fair sex as are engaged in serious occupations, let them remember that it performs the same part in beautifying domestic life as is performed by music and the fine arts in embellishing the life moral and spiritual. So long, therefore, as dress merely occupies so much time and requires so much money as we are fairly entitled to allow it, nothing can be said against it. When extravagant fashions are indulged in—extravagant habits fostered at any cost and under any circumstances—the critic is quite justified in his strictures, however severe. Dress, to be in perfect taste, need not be costly; and no woman of right feeling will adorn her person at the expense of her husband's comfort or her children's education.

"As a work of art, a well-dressed woman is a study." Her toilet will be as *bien soignée* and as well chosen at the family breakfast-table as at a ball. If she loves bright colors and can wear them with impunity, they will be as harmoniously arranged as the artist arranges his colors on the palette. If she is young, her dress will be youthful; if she is old, it will not affect simplicity. She will always follow rather than lead the prevailing fashion, and rather follow her own fashion than violate good taste or common sense.

The golden rule in dress is to avoid extremes. Do not be so original in your dress as to be peculiar; and do not affect fashions that are radically unbecoming to you. Ladies that are neither very young nor very striking in appearance cannot do better than wear quiet colors. Ladies who are not rich can always appear well dressed, with a little care in the choice and arrangement of the materials. Whatever the texture of the dress, it should be made by the very best dressmaker you can afford. As well go to a third or fourth-rate dentist, music-master, or doctor, as go to a third or fourth-rate dressmaker. The dressmaker is a woman's good or evil genius.

Morning dress should be faultless in its way. For young ladies, married or unmarried, nothing is prettier in summer than white or very light morning dresses of washing materials. Light dresses must be exquisitely fresh and clean, ribbons fresh, collars and cuffs irreproachable. All stuffs are to be rigidly eschewed except those of the very finest kind. Morning dress for elderly ladies of wealth and position should be of dark silk. Jewelry, hair ornaments, and light silk dresses are not permissible for morning wear.

Walking dress should always be quiet. Rich walking dress attracts attention, which in the street is not desirable. For the carriage, a lady may dress as elegantly as she pleases.

Elderly ladies should always dress richly. Any thin old lady may wear delicate colors, whilst a stout, florid person looks best in dark or gray. For young as well as old, the question of color must, however, be determined by complexion and figure. Rich colors harmonize with rich brunette complexions and dark hair;

delicate colors are the most suitable for delicate and fragile styles of beauty.

For ball dresses, light and diaphanous materials are worn; silk dresses are not suitable for dancing. Black and scarlet, black and violet, or white, are worn in mourning; but ladies in deep mourning should not go to balls at all. They must not dance, and their dark dresses look out of place in a gay assembly.

At dinner parties, unless of a small, friendly kind, only the fullest dress is appropriate. Demi-toilette can be worn at unceremonious dinners, and even high dresses, if the material be sufficiently rich. It is better to wear real flowers at large dinner parties, but artificial ones at balls; since the former would drop and fall to pieces with the heat and the dancing.

Much jewelry is out of place for young ladies at any time; and, indeed, there is as much propriety to be observed in the wearing of jewelry as in the wearing of dresses. Diamonds, pearls, rubies, and all transparent precious stones belong to evening dress, and should never be worn before dinner. In the morning, one's rings should be of the simplest kind, and one's jewelry limited to a good brooch, gold chain, and watch. Diamonds and pearls are as much out of place during the morning as a low dress or a wreath.

It is well to remember in the choice of jewelry that mere costliness is not always the test of value; and that an exquisite work of art, such as a fine intaglio or cameo, or a natural rarity, such as a black pearl, is a possession more *distingué* than a large brilliant which any one who has money enough can buy as well as yourself. Of all precious stones, the opal is the most lovely and commonplace. No merely vulgar woman purchases an opal.

Gloves, shoes, and boots must always be faultless. Gloves cannot be too light for the carriage, or too dark for the streets. A woman with ill-fitting gloves cannot be said to be well dressed; while to wear soiled ones at your friend's *soirée* is to show her that you think lightly of herself and her company.

It may be remarked, by the way, that perfumes should be used only in the evening, and with the strictest moderation. Perfumes, to be tolerable, must be of the most *recherché* kind. Some people, of a sensitive temperament, would be made ill by the smell of musk or patchouli.

Finally, let every lady remember Dr. Johnson's criticism on a lady's dress: "I am sure she was well dressed," said the Doctor; for I cannot remember what she had on."

THE GENTLEMAN'S TOILET.

It has been aptly said that "the bath deserves an Order." The first requisite of a gentleman's toilet is undoubtedly the bath, which should be as bracing as the constitution will allow, and used morning and evening in summer, and every day in winter. Country gentlemen, who live much in the open air, and take plenty of exercise, have no excuse for shirking the cold shower-bath; but denizens of cities, and men who are obliged to lead very sedentary lives, cannot indulge with equal safety in this luxury, and must never continue it in the teeth of reason and experience. Only physiques of finest quality can endure, much more benefit by, a cold-water shock all the year round; and though physique is always improvable, great reformation must not be attempted rashly. Let the bath of from sixty to seventy degrees be freely indulged in by the strong, and even by the less robust, in summer time; but in winter a temperature varying from eighty-five to ninety-five degrees is the safest. The flesh-brush should be vigorously applied to all parts of the body, after which the skin must be carefully dried with Turkish or huck-a-back towels. It is well to remain without clothing for some little time after bathing. Nothing is so healthy as exposure of the body to air and sun; a French physician has recommended the sun-bath as a desirable hygienic practice. A bath in fresh water should always be taken after a sea-dip.

The next thing to be done is to clean the teeth. This should be done with a good hard tooth-brush at least twice a day. Smokers should rinse the mouth immediately after smoking, and should be careful to keep the teeth scrupulously clean. The nails should also be kept exquisitely clean and short. Long nails are are an abomination.

Our advice to those who shave is, like *Punch's* advice to those about to marry—"Don't." But it must by no means be understood that suffering the beard to grow is a process that obviates all trouble. The beard should be carefully and frequently washed, well trimmed, and well combed, and the hair and whiskers kept scrupulously clean by the help of clean, stiff hair-brushes, and soap and warm water. The style of the beard should be adapted to the form of the face; but any affectation in the cut of the beard and whiskers is very objectionable, and augurs unmitigated vanity in the wearer. Long hair is never indulged in except by painters and fiddlers. The moustache should be worn neat, and not overlarge.

Beau Brummell spent two hours in dressing; but a gentleman can perform all the duties of his toilet to perfection in less than half that time.

A great French writer has said, with as much grace as philosophy, that the artist and man of letters needs only a black coat, and the absence of all pretension, to place him on the level of the best society. It must be observed, however, that this remark applies only to the intellectual workers, who, if they do occasionally commit a minor solecism in dress and manners, are forgiven on account of their fame and talents. It is not enough that a man should be clever, or well educated, or well born, to take his place in society; he must be acquainted with all that this chapter, and, indeed, this little volume throughout, professes to teach.

A gentleman should always be so well dressed that his dress shall never be remarked at all. Does this sound like an enigma? It is not meant for one. It only implies that perfect simplicity is perfect elegance, and that the true test of dress in the toilet of a gentleman is its entire harmony, unobtrusiveness, and becomingness. Displays should be avoided. Let a sensible man leave the graces and luxuries of dress to his wife, daughters, and sisters, and not seek distinction in the trinkets on his watch-chain, or the pattern of his waistcoat. To be too much in the fashion is as vulgar as to be too far behind it. No really well-bred man follows every new cut he sees in his tailor's fashion-book. Only very young men are guilty of this folly.

A man whose dress is appropriate, neat, and clean, will always look like a gentleman; but to dress appropriately, one must have a varied wardrobe. This should not, on the average, cost more than a tenth part of his income. No man can afford more than a tenth of his income for dress.

The author of *Pelham* has aptly said that "a gentleman's coat should not fit too well." There is great truth and subtlety in this observation. To be fitted too well is to look like a tailor's dummy.

In the morning, wear a frock coat, and trousers of light or dark color, as befits the season. When in the country or at the sea-side, gray or shooting costumes are best.

In the evening, though you spend it alone with your family, wear a black dress suit; and if you have sons, bring them up to do the same.

It is the observance of these trifles in domestic etiquette that marks the true gentleman. For evening parties, dinner parties, and balls wear a black dress coat, black trousers, black silk or cloth waistcoat, thin patent-leather boots, a white cravat, and white kid gloves. Abjure all fopperies, such as white silk linings, silk collars, etc.; above all, the shirt-front should be plain. At small, unceremonious parties, gloves are not necessary; but, when worn, they should be new and fit well. Economy in gloves is an insult to society. A man's jewelry should be of the best and simplest description. False jewelry, like every other form of falsehood and pretence, is unmitigated vulgarity.

Elaborate studs and sleeve-links are all foppish and vulgar. A set of good studs, a gold watch and guard, and one handsome ring, are as many ornaments as a gentleman can wear with propriety. For a ring, the man of fine taste would prefer a precious antique intaglio to the handsomest diamond or ruby that could be bought. The most elegant gentleman with whom the author was ever acquainted—a man familiar with all the courts of Europe—never wore any other shirt-studs in full dress than three valuable black pearls, each about the size of a pea, and by no means beautiful to look upon.

Lastly, a man's jewelry should always have some use, and not, like a lady's, be worn for ornament only.

Colored shirts may be worn in the morning; but they should be small in pattern and quiet in color. Fancy cloths of conspicuous patterns are exceedingly objectionable. With a colored flannel shirt always wear a white collar and wristbands. The hat should always be black; and caps and straw-hats are only admissible in summer.

If spectacles are necessary, they should be of the best and lightest make, and mounted in gold, or blue steel. For weak sight, blue or smoke-colored glasses are the best; green glasses are detestable.

A gentleman should never be seen in the street without gloves. Worsted or cotton gloves are not permissible. A man's clothes should always be well brushed, and never threadbare or shabby. No gentleman can afford to wear shabby clothes.

For the country, or the foreign tour, a gentleman will select a costume of some light woolen material, flannel shirts, thick boots, and everything to correspond. Dandyism is never more out of place than on the glacier, or among the Norwegian salmon fisheries.

There are three things one should consult in the matter of dress if one would always appear like a gentleman—viz., expense, comfort, and society. If there is one thing in this world about which we can entertain any degree of moral certainty, it is that we must pay our tailor's bills. If, therefore, our means are disproportionate to our wants, we must remember the old proverb, "Cut your coat according to your cloth," and dress as well as you possibly can upon little money.

MISCELLANEOUS;

OR,

ONE HUNDRED UNCLASSIFIED LAWS OF ETIQUETTE.

1. A GENTLEMAN must always hand a lady a chair, open the door for her to pass in or out, remove anything that may be in her way, and pick up anything she may drop, even if she is an entire stranger to him.

2. A gentleman or lady will never look over the shoulder of another who is either reading or writing.

3. No gentleman or lady will ever be guilty of personality in conversation. No wit, however keen; no sarcasm, however humorous, can make personal remarks anything but rude and vulgar.

4. A gentleman, in passing a lady where he must stand aside to give her space, must always remove his hat, and incline his head slightly.

5. A lady, in such a case, must always acknowledge the courtesy by a slight bow.

6. Exaggeration trespasses so closely upon falsehood that it is not safe to trust it. To adhere strictly to truth can never lead into error.

7. Conceit is the vice or folly of the shallow-minded; so if you would not be thought so, avoid boasting or affectations of any kind. The truly wise man is modest, and the braggart and coxcomb are valued but little.

8. It is unladylike to stand with arms a-kimbo or folded.

9. It is a mark of low breeding to fidget either with the hands or feet; to play with the watch-chain, toss the gloves, suck the head of a cane or handle of a parasol, or to fuss with a collar or necktie. Nothing is a more certain sign of gentle breeding than quiet ease without stiffness or fidgetting.

10. To swing the foot, or tap monotonously with the feet, to drum with the fingers on a table or window, are all breaches of etiquette.

11. It is ill-bred to speak of persons with whom you are but slightly acquainted by their first name.

12. No true lady will ever allow herself to speak of a gentleman by his surname without a prefix. To hear a lady talking of Holmes or Warren, instead of Mr. Holmes or Dr. Warren, gives the impression that she is low-bred.

13. No gentleman will ever criticize a wine offered to him, no matter how poor it may be. We give an instance of undaunted etiquette, which proves to what an extent a well-bred man may carry his courtesy: "In England, during the French Revolution, the Duke of Bedford invited the emigrant Duc de Grammont to a splendid dinner, one of those magnificent entertainments which Englishmen pride themselves on giving to crowned heads, and their good feeling prompts them to offer to exiles. During dessert, a bottle of Constantia was produced, which for age and flavor was supposed to be matchless. It was liquid gold in a crystal flagon—a ray of the sun descending into a goblet; it was nectar which was worthy of Jove, and in which Bacchus would

have revelled. The noble head of the house of Russell himself helped his guest to a glass of this choice wine, and de Grammont, on tasting it, declared it to be excellent. The Duke of Bedford, anxious to judge of its quality, poured out a glass, which no sooner approached his lips than, with a horrible contortion, he exclaimed: 'Why, what on earth is this?' The butler approached, took the bottle and applied it to his nostrils, and, to the dismay of his master, pronounced it to be castor-oil. The Duc de Grammont had swallowed this horrid draught without wincing."

14. Flattery is a breach of etiquette. Johnson says: "Of all wild beasts, preserve me from a tyrant; and of all tame, a flatterer."

15. No gentleman may ever break an engagement, whether it be one of business or pleasure, with a lady, or with another gentleman. If not blessed with a retentive memory, he must carry a note-book and record therein all his appointments, guarding, by frequent reference, against making two for the same day and hour. To break an engagement with a lady is almost certain to give lasting offence, and with good cause.

16. Irritability is a breach of good manners. Watts says: "To be angry about trifles is mean and childish; to rage and be furious is brutish; and to maintain perpetual wrath is akin to the practice and temper of fiends; but to prevent and suppress rising resentment is wise and glorious, is manly and divine."

17. Nothing marks a gentleman more truly than a strict punctuality. To keep another waiting is a breach of etiquette, as well as often a positive unkindness.

18. "Fine feathers make fine birds," the old proverb tells us; but no amount of fine dressing will ever *make* a lady. True politeness, gentle courtesy and refinement may be as marked in a lady wearing a calico dress and a sun-bonnet as in one in full gala dress. Mrs. Thorpe, the celebrated English authoress, tells of an interview with Mrs. Washington, than whom no more perfect lady, in the true acceptance of the term, ever lived. She says: "As Mrs. Washington was said to be so grand a lady, we thought we must put on our best bibs and bands; so we dressed ourselves in our most elegant ruffles and silks, and were introduced to her ladyship; and don't you think we found her knitting, and with her check apron on! She received us *very graciously and easily;* but

after the compliments were over, she resumed her knitting. There we were without a stitch of work, and sitting in state; but General Washington's lady, with her own hands, was knitting stockings for her husband."

19. To answer a civil question rudely, or even impatiently, is a gross breach of etiquette. Even if it inconveniences you or interrupts you, it will take no longer to answer kindly or politely than to wound or offend by crustiness.

20. No gentleman may ever refuse an apology. No matter how great the offence, how deep the resentment, an apology can never be rejected. It may not again revive friendship; but it must prevent quarrelling.

21. It is a breach of etiquette to intrude upon a business man during business hours.

22. An invalid, an elderly person, or a lady must be given the most comfortable chair in the room, must be allowed to select the light and temperature, and no true lady or gentlemen will ever object to the exercise of the privilege.

23. It is a breach of etiquette, as well as an impertinence, ever to question a child or a servant upon family affairs.

24. It is a breach of etiquette to examine a card-basket. It is true they are generally exposed in the drawing-room; but no true lady or gentleman will ever turn them over.

25. It is a breach of etiquette to consult a watch when in company. To do so, and then take leave, is an absolute impertinence, as a pleasant circle may be broken at an early hour, under the impression that "it must be late; Mr. C—— hurried away so, when he saw what time it was."

26. It is a breach of etiquette when in company to try to attract the attention of one person by signals, a cough, a poke, or a nudge. Any appearance, indeed, of privacy or mystery is rude in company.

27. It is a breach of etiquette to assume a lazy, lounging attitude in company. If any one is too weak or too ill to sit up and assume a proper position, he had better stay at home until he is stronger or in better health.

28. Mysterious allusions are rude.

29. It is a breach of etiquette, in general conversation, to refer to incidents known to only one of the company, thus forcing a

species of *tête-a-tête*, and withdrawing a perhaps unwilling partner from the general society.

30. Cards of ceremony must be answered either by a call, a letter, or a return card, within a week after their reception.

31. New-Year's calls must be made in person. It is a breach of etiquette to send a card, unless prevented by illness from calling.

32. Never rise to take leave in the midst of an interesting conversation; wait until there is a pause, and then withdraw, with as little disturbance as possible.

33. If you are calling, and another person enters, never offer the chair assigned you by the lady of the house; it is her privilege to decide where to place her guests, and an impertinence on your part to usurp her place.

34. A gentleman will never talk of his business affairs to a lady, nor a lady weary her gentlemen friends by an account of her domestic affairs.

35. The only gifts that may be offered or accepted between ladies and gentlemen who are not related or engaged are books, flowers, music, or confectionery. A lady who accepts costly presents of jewelry puts herself under an obligation that she may find troublesome, and no true gentleman will expose a lady to the pain of refusing an improper gift of this kind.

36. In entering a room filled with people, it is etiquette to bow slightly, as a general salutation, before speaking to each of those assembled.

37. It is etiquette, before taking a place at table, to say "Good-morning," or "Good-evening," to those in the room before you, and especially to those who preside over the meal.

38. It is a breach of etiquette to go into company with the breath tainted by eating onions, garlic, cheese, or any other strong-scented food.

39. It is a breach of etiquette for a gentleman to enter a lady's presence smelling of tobacco or wine.

40. It is a breach of etiquette to send a present hoping for another.

41. It is a breach of etiquette ever to refer to a gift you have made, a favor you have granted, or an obligation of any kind under which another lies with regard to you.

42. It is a breach of etiquette, and shows a sad want of true

delicacy, to return a gift very soon. An obligation of that kind, if accepted at all, must not be thrust back at once in the donor's face.

43. It is a breach of etiquette for a husband or wife to speak of each other by their initial letter. When you hear a lady saying, "B., gave me this," or a gentleman saying, "I always refer such matters to Mrs. P.," you may rest assured, whatever their social station, they are low-bred.

44. "Civility," says Lord Chesterfield, "is particularly due to all women; and remember that no provocation whatsoever can justify any man in not being civil to every woman; and the greatest man would justly be reckoned a brute if he were not civil to the meanest woman. It is due to their sex, and is the only protection they have against the superior strength of ours."

45. Too great familiarity towards a new acquaintance is a breach of etiquette. You are less likely to offend by being too ceremonious.

46. To notice, by look or word, any deformity, any scar or misfortune to the face or figure of a friend, is not only a breach of etiquette of the grossest kind, but is a want of humanity and good feeling as well.

47. It is a breach of etiquette, when offering a gift, to represent it as valueless, or useless to yourself. "If you do not have it, the pigs will," is a homely old proverb in such cases, not acceptable in polite society.

48. It is a breach of etiquette to laugh at your own wit. If others will not do that for you, you had better let your remark pass unnoticed.

49. It is a breach of etiquette to lean heavily upon a table; and also to tip a chair to and fro when you are talking; and you will be justly punished if you find yourself sprawling on the floor with the chair on top of you.

50. It is a breach of etiquette to write your own remarks in a borrowed book.

51. *Scolding* is ill-bred.

52. It is a breach of etiquette for a gentleman to keep his hat on when handing a lady to a carriage.

53. The man who will insult his inferiors is a boor at heart,

however polished he may appear amongst his equals, or however deferential to his superiors.

54. It is a breach of etiquette to display any bashfulness in company. Lord Chesterfield says: "As for the *mauvaise honte*, I hope you are above it. Your figure is like other people's; I suppose you will care that your dress shall be so too, and to avoid any singularity. What, then, should you be ashamed of? And why not go into a mixed company with as much ease and as little concern as you would go into your own room? Vice and ignorance are the only things I know which one ought to be ashamed of; keep clear of them, and you may go anywhere without fear or concern. I have known some people who, from feeling the pain and inconvenience of this *mauvaise honte*, have rushed into the other extreme, and turned impudent, as cowards sometimes grow desperate from the excess of danger; but this, too, is carefully to be avoided, there being nothing more generally shocking than impudence. The medium between the two extremes marks out the well-bred man; he feels himself firm and easy in all companies; is modest without being bashful, and steady without being impudent; if he is a stranger, he observes with care the manners and ways of the people most esteemed at that place, and conforms to them with complaisance."

55. It is a breach of etiquette to wear an air of abstraction in society. If your mind is really so absorbed that you cannot pay attention to what is going on around you, you had better stay at home. An absent mind is much more frequently a proof of self-conceit than of genius.

56. Eccentricity of any kind is in bad taste.

57. To imitate the manners, voice, attitude, or gestures of great men were a folly almost too absurd to mention if it were not so common. Many persons, from a real or fancied personal resemblance to some celebrity, will ape their manners also, as if mere appearance would make them equally distinguished.

58. It is wiser, if you have met with reverses, to withdraw yourself from society than to have society withdraw from you.

59. It is a breach of etiquette to assume pedantic airs; to talk of the Latin and Greek authors, and quote in those languages.

60. It is a breach of etiquette to make a quotation in a foreign language and then translate it, thereby giving your listeners to

understand that you do not consider them as well informed as yourself.

61. Shakespeare says:

> "To thine own self be true,
> And it must follow, as the night the day,
> Thou canst not then be false to any man."

62. It is a gross breach of etiquette to contradict any one.

63. The man who would suffer himself to speak a word against a woman, or to rail at women generally, deserves a rebuke recently given to a coxcomb at an English dinner-party, who was checked in his loud abuse of the sex by one of the company, who said: "I hope it is the gentleman's own mother and sisters who are referred to, and not ours."

64. If you try to make yourself appear more important than you really are, you run the risk of being considered less so.

65. Marston says: "I, me, and mine, should be bowed out of genteel circles. Egotism adorns no one."

66. It is a breach of etiquette to offer a partner in dancing an ungloved hand.

67. Spitting is as vulgar as it is disgusting.

68. "The scholar, without good breeding, is a pedant; the philosopher, a cynic; the soldier, a brute; and every man disagreeable," says Chesterfield.

69. It is a gross breach of etiquette to betray an implied or involuntary confidence, even if you have not been bound to secresy.

70. Bishop Beveridge says: "Never speak of a man's virtues before his face, nor of his faults behind his back."

71. "In private, watch your thoughts; in your family, watch your temper; in society, watch your tongue."

72. "To arrive at the heart of true courtesy," says a modern writer, "separate the old English titles for the well-bred; they were the *gentle*-man and *gentle*-woman."

73. It is better to live alone than in low company. If you cannot keep good company, keep none.

74. Sterne thus defines courtship: "True courtship consists in a number of quiet, gentlemanly attentions; not so pointed as to alarm, not so vague as to be misunderstood."

75. It is a breach of etiquette to enter a room noisily, slamming the door, or stamping heavily upon the floor.

76. It is a breach of etiquette to make violent or abrupt movements.

77. It is a breach of etiquette to neglect calling upon your friends. "Visiting," says a French writer, "forms the chord which binds society together, and it is so firmly tied that were the knot severed, society would perish."

78. It is a breach of etiquette to select the route when walking with a lady, unless she has requested you to do so.

79. It is ill-bred to refuse the last piece on the plate or dish, if it is offered to you, as it implies a fear that there is no more in the pantry.

80. It is a breach of etiquette to undertake any commission for a friend and neglect to perform it. Forgetfulness is no excuse.

81. It is a breach of etiquette to answer a serious remark by a flippant one.

82. Practical joking is a breach of etiquette that cannot be too severely censured.

83. It is a breach of etiquette to read when there is any other person present. In the family circle, a member who opens a book should apologize for and explain his apparent rudeness, if obliged to study or refer to the volume.

84. It is a breach of etiquette to yawn.

85. It is a breach of etiquette to blow the nose loudly.

86. It is a breach of etiquette to suck the teeth.

87. It is a breach of etiquette to pick the teeth or clean the nails in company.

88. It is a breach of etiquette to speak much of your own performances.

89. It is a gross breach of etiquette to pass between two persons who are conversing together.

90. It is a breach of etiquette to pass *before* anybody. If actually necessary, it must be done with an apology.

91. It is a breach of etiquette to urge wine upon a guest who has already declined to drink.

92. It is a breach of etiquette to write a letter of congratulation upon mourning paper, even if it is habitually used.

93. It is a breach of etiquette to call a new acquaintance by the Christian name, unless requested to do so.

94. If you write requesting an autograph, it is a breach of etiquette to omit to enclose a postage-stamp for the reply.

95. Ladies should avoid the use of strong perfumes. They are unpleasant to nauseating to some persons; and it is a breach of etiquette to annoy other people.

96. It is a breach of etiquette to lend a borrowed book, unless you have the special permission of the owner to do so.

97. It is a breach of etiquette, as well as a most dangerous experiment, to recommend remedies to an invalid who is under the care of a physician.

98. A lady commits a breach of etiquette that amounts to a gross impropriety by calling upon a gentleman, excepting upon business, at his place of business. Even relatives, unless in the immediate family, cannot receive calls from ladies at home.

99. Gentlemen should never stand upon the hearthrug with their backs to the fire, either in a friend's house or their own.

100. Forgetfulness is a breach of etiquette. It is impossible to be polite without cultivating a good memory. The absent or self-absorbed person who forgets the names of his next-door neighbors, recalls unlucky topics, confuses the personal relationships of his personal friends, speaks of the dead as if they were still living, talks of people in their hearing, and commits a hundred such blunders without any malevolent intention, is sure to make enemies for himself, and to wound the feelings of others. Carelessness, carried to a certain pitch, becomes unchristian. "It is not well," says an old proverb, "to talk of the gallows to a man whose father was hanged." Some persons are so notoriously absent or forgetful, that their friends will say of them: "We must not tell B——; he is certain to tread on somebody's corns. We must ask him some evening when we are alone."

DICK & FITZGERALD,

PUBLISHERS, NEW YORK.

*** The Publishers, upon receipt of the price, will send any of the following books by mail, POSTAGE FREE, to any part of the United States. In ordering books, the full name, post office, county and State should be plainly written.

Wilson's Book of Recitations and Dialogues. With Instructions in Elocution and Declamation. Containing a choice selection of Poetical and Prose Recitations and Original Colloquies. Designed as a Reading Book for Classes, and as an Assistant to Teachers and Students in preparing Exhibitions. By FLOYD B. WILSON, Professor of Elocution. This collection has been prepared with a special view to the development of the two cardinal principles of true Elocution—Voice and Action, and include a large proportion of Recitations and Dialogues, which appear for the first time in this form. The Colloquies are entirely original.
Paper covers. Price..**30 cts.**
Bound in boards, cloth back..**50 cts.**

Frost's Dialogues for Young Folks. A collection of Original Moral and Humorous Dialogues. Adapted to the use of School and Church Exhibitions, Family Gatherings, and Juvenile Celebrations on all Occasions. By S. A. FROST, author of "Frost's Original Letter Writer," etc. This collection of Dialogues is just what has long been wanted—it contains a variety that will suit every taste; some of the subjects are humorous, some satirical, hitting at the follies of vice and fashion, while others are pathetic, and all are entertaining. A few of the Dialogues are long enough to form a sort of little drama that will interest more advanced scholars, while short and easy ones abound for the use of quite young children. Most of the Dialogues introduce two or three characters only, but some require a greater number. The subjects chosen will, it is hoped, be found useful in conveying sound moral instruction as well as giving the opportunity to display memory and vivacity in rendering them.
Paper covers. Price..**30 cts.**
Bound in boards, cloth back, side in colors..**50 cts.**

The Parlor Stage. A Collection of Drawing-Room Proverbs, Charades and Tableaux Vivants. By Miss S. A. FROST. The authoress of this attractive volume has performed her task with skill, talent, and we might say, with genius; for the Acting Charades and Proverbs are really minor dramas of a high order of merit. There are twenty-four of them, and fourteen *Tableaux*, all of which are excellent. The characters are admirably drawn, well contrasted, and the plots and dialogues much better than those of many popular pieces performed at the public theatres. Any parlor with folding or sliding doors is suitable for their representation (or, if there are no sliding or folding doors, a temporary curtain will answer). The dresses are all those of modern society, and the scenery and properties can be easily provided from the resources of almost any family residence in town or country. The book is elegantly got up, and we commend it heartily to young gentlemen and ladies who wish to beguile the long winter evenings with a species of amusement at once interesting, instructive and amusing.
368 pages, small 8vo, cloth, gilt side and back, beveled edges. Price..**$1 50.**

The Young Debater and Chairman's Assistant. Containing instructions how to form and conduct Societies, Clubs and other organized associations. Also, full Rules of Order for the government of their Business and Debates; together with complete directions How to Compose Resolutions, Reports and Petitions; and the best way to manage Public Meetings, Celebrations, Dinners and Pic-Nics. Also instructions in Elocution, with hints on Debate. This book is compiled from our larger work entitled "The Finger Post to Public Business." To any one who desires to become familiar with the duties of an Officer or Committee-man in a Society or Association, this work will be invaluable, as it contains minute instructions in everything that pertains to the routine of Society Business. 152 pages. Paper cover, price..**30 cts.**
Bound in boards, with cloth back, price..**50 cts.**

Frost's Laws and By-Laws of American Society. A condensed but thorough treatise on Etiquette and its usages in America. Containing plain and reliable directions for deportment on the following subjects: Letters of Introduction, Salutes and Salutations, Calls, Conversations, Invitations, Dinner Company, Balls, Morning and Evening Parties, Visiting, Street Etiquette, Riding and Driving, Travelling; Etiquette in Church, Etiquette for Places of Amusement; Servants, Hotel Etiquette; Etiquette in Weddings, Baptisms, and Funerals; Etiquette with Children, and at the Card-Table; Visiting Cards, Letter-Writing, the Lady's Toilet, the Gentleman's Toilet; besides one hundred unclassified laws applicable to all occasions. Paper cover, price..**30 cts.**
Bound in boards, with cloth back, price..**50 cts.**

How to Cook Potatoes, Apples, Eggs and Fish, Four Hundred Different Ways. The matter embraced in this work consists of the combined contents of four little books which have obtained immense popularity in France and England, and which have been thoroughly revised and adapted for American housekeepers by an American cook of great experience. The work especially recommends itself to those who are often embarrassed for want of variety in dishes suitable for the breakfast table or, on occasions where the necessity arises for preparing a meal at short notice.
Paper covers, price..**30 cts.**
Bound in boards, with cloth back, price..**50 cts.**

Uncle Josh's Trunk-Full of Fun. A portfolio of first-class Wit and Humor, and never-ending source of Jollity, Containing the richest collection of Comical Stories, Cruel Sells, Side-splitting Jokes, Humorous Poetry, Quaint Parodies, Burlesque Sermons, New Conundrums and Mirth Provoking Speeches ever published. Interspersed with Curious Puzzles, Amusing Card Tricks, and Feats of Parlor Magic. Illustrated with nearly 200 Funny Engravings. This book consists of 64 large octavo pages, and contains three times as much reading matter and real fun as any other book of the same price. Illustrated cover, printed in colors, price...**15 cts.**

The American Housewife and Kitchen Directory. This valuable book embraces three hundred and seventy-eight receipts for cooking all sorts of American dishes in the most economical manner, and, besides these, it also contains a great variety of important secrets for washing, cleansing, scouring, and extracting grease, paints, stains and iron-mould from cloth, muslin and linen.
Bound in ornamental paper covers, price..**30 cts.**
Bound in boards, with cloth back, price..**50 cts.**

How to Cook and How to Carve. Giving plain and easily understood directions for preparing and cooking, with the greatest economy, every kind of dish, with complete instructions for serving the same. This book is just the thing for a young Housekeeper. It explains everything about the art of Cooking. It is worth a dozen of expensive French books.
Paper covers, price..**30 cts.**
Bound in boards, with cloth back, price..**50 cts.**

Howard's Book of Conundrums and Riddles. Containing over 1,400 Witty Conundrums, Queer Riddles, Perplexing Puzzles. Ingenious Enigmas, Clever Charades, Curious Catches, and Amusing Sells, original and newly dressed. This splendid collection of curious paradoxes will afford the material for a never-ending feast of fun and amusement. Any person, with the assistance of this book, may take the lead in entertaining a company and keeping them in roars of laughter for hours together. It is an invaluable companion for a Pic-nic, or Summer Excursion of any kind, and is just the thing to make a fireside circle merry on a long winter's evening. There is not a poor riddle in the book, the majority being fresh and of the highest order. Paper cover, price.................30 cts.
Bound in boards, cloth back, price.....................................50 cts.

Frost's Book of Tableaux and Shadow Pantomimes. Containing a choice collection of Tableaux or Living Pictures, embracing Moving Tableaux, Mother Goose Tableaux, Fairy Tale Tableaux, Charade and Proverb Tableaux; together with directions for arranging the stage, costuming the characters, and forming appropriate groups. By Miss S. Annie Frost. To which is added a number of Shadow Acts and Pantomimes, with complete stage instructions. 180 pages, paper cover...30 cts.
Bound in boards, cloth back...50 cts.

How to Amuse an Evening Party. A complete collection of Home Recreations, including Round Games, Forfeits, Parlor Magic, Puzzles, and Comic Diversions; together with a great variety of Scientific Recreations and Evening Amusements. Profusely illustrated with nearly 200 fine wood-cuts Paper, price.......................................30 cts.
Bound in boards, ornamental...50 cts.

Laughing Gas. An Encyclopædia of Wit, Wisdom, and Wind. By Sam Slick, Jr. Comically illustrated with 100 original and laughable Engravings, and nearly 500 side-extending Jokes, and other things to get fat on; and the best thing of it is, that everything about the book is new and fresh—all new—new designs, new stories, new type—no comic almanac stuff. Price...25 cts.

The Egyptian Dream Book and Fortune-Teller. Containing an Alphabetical List of Dreams, and numerous methods of Telling Fortunes, including the celebrated Oraculum of Napoleon Bonaparte. Illustrated with explanatory diagrams. 16mo, boards, cloth back.
Price...40 Cts.

Ned Turner's Black Jokes. A collection of Funny Stories, Jokes, and Conundrums, interspersed with Witty Sayings and Humorous Dialogues. As given by Ned Turner, the Celebrated Ethiopian Delineator and Equestrian Clown. Price..10 cts.

Book of 1,000 Tales and Amusing Adventures. Containing over 300 Engravings, and 450 pages. This is a magnificent book, and is crammed full of narratives and adventures. Price..........$1 50

The Game of Whist. Rules, Directions, and Maxims to be observed in playing it. Containing, also, Primary Rules for Beginners, Explanations and Directions for Old Players, and the Laws of the Game. Compiled from Hoyle and Matthews. Price.........................12 cts.

10,000 Wonderful Things. Comprising the Marvellous and Rare, Odd, Curious, Quaint, Eccentric, and Extraordinary in all Ages and Nations, in Art, Nature, and Science, including many Wonders of the World, enriched with hundreds of authentic illustrations. 16mo, cloth, gilt side and back. Price...$1 50

Brudder Bones' Book of Stump Speeches and Burlesque Orations. Also containing Humorous Lectures, Ethiopian Dialogues, Plantation Scenes, Negro Farces and Burlesques, Laughable Interludes and Comic Recitations, interspersed with Dutch, Irish, French and Yankee Stories. Compiled and edited by JOHN F. SCOTT. This book contains some of the best hits of the leading negro delineators of the present time, as well as mirth-provoking jokes and repartees of the most celebrated End-Men of the day, and specially designed for the introduction of fun in an evening's entertainment. Paper covers. Price.............................**30 cts.**
Bound in boards, illuminated...**50 cts.**

Frost's Original Letter-Writer. A complete collection of Original Letters and Notes, upon every imaginable subject of Every-Day Life, with plain directions about everything connected with writing a letter. Containing Letters of Introduction, Letters on Business, Letters answering Advertisements, Letters of Recommendation, Applications for Employment, Letters of Congratulation, of Condolence, of Friendship and Relationship, Love Letters, Notes of Invitation, Notes Accompanying Gifts, Letters of Favor, of Advice, and Letters of Excuse, together with an appropriate answer to each. The whole embracing three hundred letters and notes. By S. A. FROST, author of "The Parlor Stage," "Dialogues for Young Folks," etc. To which is added a comprehensive Table of Synonyms alone worth double the price asked for the book. This work is not a rehash of English writers, but is entirely practical and original, and suited to the wants of the American public. We assure our readers that it is the best collection of letters ever published in this country. Bound in boards, cloth back, with illuminated sides. Price..**50 cts.**

Inquire Within *for Anything you Want to Know; or, Over 3,700 Facts for the People.* "Inquire Within" is one of the most valuable and extraordinary volumes ever presented to the American public, and embodies nearly 4,000 facts, in most of which any person will find instruction, aid and entertainment. It contains so many valuable recipes, that an enumeration of them requires *seventy-two columns of fine type for the index.* Illustrated. 436 large pages. Price........................**$1 50**

The Sociable; *or, One Thousand and One Home Amusements.* Containing Acting Proverbs, Dramatic Charades, Acting Charades, Tableaux Vivants, Parlor Games and Parlor Magic, and a choice collection of Puzzles, etc., illustrated with nearly 300 Engravings and Diagrams, the whole being a fund of never-ending entertainment. By the author of the "Magician's Own Book." Nearly 400 pages, 12 mo. cloth, gilt side stamp. Price..**$1 50**

Martine's Hand-Book of Etiquette and Guide to True Politeness. A complete Manual for all those who desire to understand good breeding, the customs of good society, and to avoid incorrect and vulgar habits. Containing clear and comprehensive directions for correct manners, conversation, dress, introductions, rules for good behavior at Dinner Parties and the table, with hints on wine and carving at the table; together with Etiquette of the Ball and Assembly Room, Evening Parties, and the usages to be observed when visiting or receiving calls; deportment in the street and when travelling. To which is added the Etiquette of Courtship and Marriage. Bound in boards, with cloth back. Price................**50 cts.**
Bound in cloth, gilt side..**75 cts.**

Day's American Ready-Reckoner, containing Tables for rapid calculations of Aggregate Values, Wages, Salaries, Board, Interest Money, &c., &c. Also, Tables of Timber, Plank, Board and Log Measurements, with full explanations how to measure them, either by the square foot (board measure), cubic foot (timber measure), &c. Bound in boards. Price...**50 cts.**
Bound in cloth...**75 cts.**

The American Home Cook Book. Containing several hundred excellent Recipes. The whole based on many years' experience of an American Housewife. Illustrated with Engravings. All the Recipes in this book are written from actual experiments in Cooking. There are no copyings from theoretical cooking recipes.
Bound in boards, cloth back. Price..................................50 cts.
Bound in paper covers. Price..30 cts.

Amateur Theatricals and Fairy-Tale Dramas. A collection of original plays, expressly designed for Drawing-room performance. By S. A. Frost. This work is designed to meet a want, which has been long felt, of short and amusing pieces suitable to the limited stage of the private parlor. The old friends of fairy-land will be recognized among the Fairy-Tale Dramas, newly clothed and arranged.
Paper covers. Price..30 cts.
Bound in boards, with cloth back......................................50 cts.

Parlor Tricks with Cards. Containing explanations of Tricks and Deceptions with Playing Cards, embracing Tricks with Cards performed by Sleight-of-hand, by the aid of Memory, Mental Calculation and Arrangement of the Cards, by the aid of Confederacy; and Tricks performed by the aid of Prepared Cards. The whole illustrated and made plain and easy, with 70 engravings. This book is an abridgment of our large work, entitled "The Secret Out."
Paper covers. Price..30 cts.
Bound in boards, with cloth back......................................50 cts.

Chesterfield's Letter-writer and Complete Book of Etiquette; *or, Concise, Systematic Directions for Arranging and Writing Letters.* Also, Model Correspondence in Friendship and Business, and a great variety of Model Love Letters. This work is also a Complete Book of Etiquette. There is more real information in this book than in half a dozen volumes of the most expensive ones.
Bound in boards, with cloth back. Price...........................35 cts.

Frank Converse's Complete Banjo Instructor. Without a Master. Containing a choice collection of Banjo Solos, Hornpipes, Reels, Jigs, Walk Arounds, Songs, and Banjo Stories, progressively arranged and plainly explained. Bound in boards, with cloth back. Price.......50 cts.

The Magician's Own Book. Containing several hundred amusing Sleight-of-hand and Card Tricks, Perplexing Puzzles, Entertaining Tricks and Secret Writing Explained. Illustrated with over 500 wood engravings. 12mo., cloth, gilt side and back stamp. Price..........$1 50

North's Book of Love Letters. With Directions how to write and when to use them, and 120 specimen Letters, suitable for Lovers of any age and condition, and under all circumstances. Interspersed with the author's comments thereon. The whole forming a convenient handbook of valuable information and counsel for the use of those who need friendly guidance and advice in matters of Love, Courtship and Marriage. By Ingoldsby North. This book is recommended to all who are from any cause in doubt as to the manner in which they should write or reply to letters upon love and courtship. The reader will be aided in his thoughts—he will see where he is likely to please and where to displease, how to begin and how to end his letter, and how to judge of those nice shades of expression and feeling concerning which a few mistaken expressions may create misunderstanding. All who wish not only to copy a love letter, but to learn the art of writing them, will find North's book a very pleasant, sensible and friendly companion. It is an additional recommendation that the variety offered is very large. Cloth. Price.....................................75 cts.
Bound in boards..50 cts.

The Parlor Magician; *or, One Hundred Tricks for the Drawing-Room*, containing an Extensive and Miscellaneous Collection of Conjuring and Legerdemain; Sleights with Dice, Dominoes, Cards, Ribbons, Rings, Fruit, Coin, Balls, Handkerchiefs, etc., all of which may be performed in the Parlor or Drawing-Room, without the aid of any apparatus; also embracing a choice variety of Curious Deceptions, which may be performed with the aid of simple apparatus; the whole illustrated and clearly explained with 121 engravings. Paper Covers. Price................30 cts.
Bound in boards, with cloth back....................................50 cts.

Book of Riddles and Five Hundred Home Amusements. Containing a Choice and Curious Collection of Riddles, Charades, Enigmas, Rebuses, Anagrams, Transpositions, Conundrums, Amusing Puzzles, Queer Sleights, Recreations in Arithmetic, Fireside Games and Natural Magic, embracing Entertaining Amusements in Magnetism, Chemistry, Second Sight and Simple Recreations in Science for Family and Social Pastime, illustrated with sixty Engravings. Paper covers. Price............30 cts.
Bound in boards, with cloth back....................................50 cts.

Book of Fireside Games. Containing an Explanation of the most Entertaining Games suited to the Family Circle as a Recreation, such as Games of Action, Games which merely require attention, Games which require memory, Catch Games, which have for their objects Tricks or Mystification, Games in which an opportunity is afforded to display Gallantry, Wit, or some slight knowledge of certain Sciences, Amusing Forfeits, Fireside Games for Winter Evening Amusement, etc.
Paper covers. Price...30 cts.
Bound in boards, with cloth back....................................50 cts.

Parlor Theatricals; *or, Winter Evenings' Entertainment.* Containing Acting Proverbs, Dramatic Charades, Acting Charades, or Drawing-Room Pantomimes, Musical Burlesques, Tableaux Vivants, etc.; with Instructions for Amateurs; how to Construct a Stage and Curtain; how to get up Costumes and Properties; on the "Making up" of Characters; Exits and Entrances; how to arrange Tableaux, etc. Illustrated with Engravings. Paper covers. Price......................................30 cts.
Bound in boards, cloth back...50 cts.

The Book of 500 Curious Puzzles. Containing a large collection of entertaining Paradoxes, Perplexing Deceptions in numbers, and Amusing Tricks in Geometry. By the author of "The Sociable," "The Secret Out," "The Magician's Own Book." Illustrated with a great variety of Engravings. This book commands a large sale. It will furnish fun and amusement for a whole winter. Paper covers. Price..............30 cts.
Bound in boards, with cloth back....................................50 cts.

The above five books are compiled from the "Sociable" and "Magician's Own."

The American Boys' Book of Sports and Games. A Repository of In and Out-Door Amusements for Boys and Youth. Illustrated with nearly 700 engravings, designed by White, Herrick, Weir and Harvey, and engraved by N. Orr. This is, unquestionably, the most attractive and valuable book of its kind ever issued in this or any other country. It has been three years in preparation, and embraces all the sports and games that tend to develop the physical constitution, improve the mind and heart, and relieve the tedium of leisure hours, both in the parlor and the field. The Engravings are all in the finest style of art, and embrace eight full-page ornamental titles, illustrating the several departments of the work, beautifully printed on tinted paper. The book is issued in the best style, being printed on fine sized paper, and handsomely bound. Extra cloth, gilt side and back, extra gold. Price...$3 50
Extra cloth, full gilt edges, back and side.........................$4 00

Spencer's Book of Comic Speeches and Humorous Recitations. A collection of Comic Speeches and Dialogues, Humorous Prose and Poetical Recitations, Laughable Dramatic Scenes and Burlesques, and Eccentric Characteristic Soliloquies and Stories. Suitable for School Exhibitions and Evening Entertainments. Edited by ALBERT J. SPENCER. This is the best book of Comic Recitations that has ever been published, and commands a large sale on account of its real merit. It is crammed full of Comic Poetry, Laughable Lectures, Irish and Dutch Stories, Yankee Yarns, Negro Burlesques, Short Dramatic Scenes, Humorous Dialogues, and all kinds of Funny Speeches.
Paper covers. Price..**30 cts.**
Bound in boards, cloth back..**50 cts.**

Marache's Manual of Chess. Containing a description of the Board and the Pieces, Chess Notation, Technical Terms with diagrams illustrating them, Relative Value of the Pieces, Laws of the Game, General Observations on the Pieces, Preliminary Games for Beginners, Fifty Openings of Games, giving all the latest discoveries of Modern Masters, with best games and copious notes. Twenty Endings of Games, showing easiest ways of effecting Checkmate. Thirty-six ingenious Diagram Problems, and Sixteen curious Chess Stratagems. To which is added a Treatise on the Games of Backgammon, Russian Backgammon and Dominoes, the whole being one of the best Books for Beginners ever published. By N. MARACHE, Chess Editor of "Wilkes' Spirit of the Times."
Bound in boards, cloth back. Price..**50 cts.**
Cloth, gilt side..**75 cts.**

Martine's Sensible Letter Writer; Being a comprehensive and complete Guide and Assistant for those who desire to carry on Epistolary Correspondence; Containing a large collection of model letters, on the simplest matters of life, adapted to all ages and conditions,

EMBRACING,

Business Letters;
Applications for Employment, with Letters of Recommendation, and Answers to Advertisements;
Letters between Parents and Children;
Letters of Friendly Counsel and Remonstrance;
Letters soliciting Advice, Assistance and Friendly Favors;
Letters of Courtesy, Friendship and Affection;
Letters of Condolence and Sympathy;
A Choice Collection of Love Letters, for Every Situation in a Courtship;
Notes of Ceremony, Familiar Invitations, etc., together with Notes of Acceptance and Regret.

The whole containing 300 Sensible Letters and Notes. This is an invaluable book for those persons who have not had sufficient practice to enable them to write letters without great effort. It contains such a variety of letters, that models may be found to suit every subject. Bound in boards, with illuminated cover and cloth back, 207 pages. Price............**50 cts.**
Bound in cloth..**75 cts.**

The Perfect Gentleman. A book of Etiquette and Eloquence. Containing Information and Instruction for those who desire to become brilliant or conspicuous in General Society, or at Parties, Dinners, or Popular Gatherings, etc. It gives directions how to use wine at table, with Rules for judging the quality thereof, Rules for Carving, and a complete Etiquette of the Dinner Table, including Dinner Speeches, Toasts and Sentiments, Wit and Conversation at Table, etc. It has also an American Code of Etiquette and Politeness for all occasions. Model Speeches, with Directions how to deliver them. Duties of the Chairman at Public Meetings. Forms of Preambles and Resolutions, etc. It is a handsomely bound and gilt volume of 335 pages.
Price..**$1 50**

Hillgrove's Ball-room Guide and Complete Dancing-master. Containing a plain treatise on Etiquette and Deportment at Balls and Parties, with valuable hints on Dress and the Toilet, together with full explanations of the Rudiments, Terms, Figures and Steps used in Dancing, including clear and precise instructions how to dance all kinds of Quadrilles, Waltzes, Polkas, Redowas, Reels, Round, Plain and Fancy Dances, so that any person may learn them without the aid of a teacher; to which is added, easy directions for calling out the Figures of every dance, and the amount of Music required for each. The whole illustrated with 176 descriptive engravings and diagrams. By THOMAS HILLGROVE, Professor of Dancing.
Bound in cloth, with gilt side and back. Price........................**$1 00**
Bound in boards, cloth back..**75 cts.**

Wright's Book of 3,000 American Receipts; *or, Light-House of Valuable Information.* Containing over 3,000 Receipts in all the Useful and Domestic Arts—including Cooking, Confectionery, Distilling, Perfumery, Chemicals, Varnishes, Dyeing, Agriculture, etc. Embracing valuable secrets that cannot be obtained from any other source. No exertion or expense has been spared to make this work as comprehensive and accurate as possible. Many Receipts will be found in it that have never before appeared in print in this country. Some idea may be formed of its value in the latter respect, when it is stated that the compiler has been for many years engaged in collecting rare and valuable Receipts from numerous languages besides the English. This is by far the most valuable American Receipt Book that has ever been published.
12mo., cloth, 359 pages. Price..**$1 50**

The Modern Pocket Hoyle. Containing all the Games of Skill and Chance, as played in this country at the present time; being an "authority on all disputed points." By "TRUMPS." This valuable manual is all original, or thoroughly revised, from the best and latest authorities, and includes the laws and complete directions for playing one hundred and eleven different games, comprising Card games, Chess, Checkers, Dominoes, Backgammon, Dice, Billiards, and all the Field Games. 388 pages.
Paper covers. Price..**50 cts.**
Bound in boards, cloth back..**75 cts.**
Bound in cloth, gilt side and back..................................**$1 25**

Richardson's Monitor of Free-Masonry. A Complete Guide to the various Ceremonies and Routine in Free-Mason's Lodges, Chapters, Encampments, Hierarchies, etc., in all the Degrees, whether Modern, Ancient, Ineffable, Philosophical or Historical. Containing, also, the Signs, Tokens, Grips, Pass-words, Decorations, Drapery, Dress, Regalia and Jewels, in each Degree. Profusely illustrated with Explanatory Engravings, Plans of the Interior of Lodges, etc. By JABEZ RICHARDSON, A. M. A book of 185 pages.
Bound in paper covers. Price.......................................**50 cts.**
Bound and gilt...**$1 00**

Rarey and Knowlson's Complete Horse-tamer and Farrier. A New and Improved Edition, containing Mr. Rarey's whole Secret of Subduing and Breaking Vicious Horses, together with his Improved Plan of Managing Young Colts, and breaking them to the Saddle, the Harness and the Sulky, with Rules for selecting a good Horse, for Feeding Horses, etc. Also, THE COMPLETE FARRIER; or, Horse Doctor; a Guide for the Treatment of Horses in all Diseases to which that noble animal is liable, being the result of fifty years' extensive practice of the author, JOHN C. KNOWLSON, during his life an English Farrier of high popularity, containing the latest discoveries in the Cure of Spavin. Illustrated with descriptive Engravings.
Bound in boards, cloth back. Price.................................**50 cts.**

Book of Household Pets. Containing valuable instructions about the Diseases, Breeding, Training and Management of the Canary, Mocking Bird, Brown Thrush, or Thrasher, and other birds, and the rearing and management of all kinds of Pigeons and Fancy Poultry, Rabbits, Squirrels, Guinea Pigs, White Mice, and Dogs; together with a Comprehensive Treatise on the Principle and Management of the Salt and Fresh Water Aquarium. Illustrated with 123 fine wood-cuts.
Bound in boards. Price..**50 cts.**
Bound in cloth, gilt side..**75 cts.**

Athletic Sports for Boys. A Repository of Graceful Recreations for Youth, containing clear and complete instructions in Gymnastics, Limb Exercises. Jumping, Pole Leaping, Dumb Bells, Indian Clubs, Parallel Cars, the Horizontal Bar, the Trapeze, the Suspended Ropes, Skating, Swimming, Rowing, Sailing, Horsemanship, Riding, Driving, Angling, Fencing and Broadsword. The whole splendidly illustrated with 194 fine wood-cuts and diagrams.
Bound in boards, with cloth back. Price............................**75 cts.**
Bound in cloth, gilt side..**$1 00**

The Play-Room; *or, In-Door Games for Boys and Girls;* including Round Games and Forfeits, Slate and Board Games; also numerous Table and Toy Games, together with a large collection of Evening Amusements, Comprehending Comic Diversions, Parlor Magic, Tricks with Cards, Scientific Recreations and Puzzles. Profusely illustrated with 197 fine wood cuts. Bound in boards, with cloth back. Price......................**50 cts.**
Bound in cloth, gilt side..**75 cts.**

The Play-Ground; *or, Out-Door Games for Boys.* A Book of Healthy Recreations for Youth, containing over a hundred Amusements, including Games of Activity and Speed; Games with Toys, Marbles, Tops, Hoops, Kites. Archery, Balls; with Cricket, Croquet and Base-Ball. Illustrated with 124 wood-cuts. Bound in boards. Price................**50 cts.**
Bound in cloth, gilt side..**75 cts.**

The above four books are abridged from the "American Boy's Book of Sports and Games."

The Young Reporter; *or, How to Write Short-Hand.* A complete Phonographic Teacher, intended to afford thorough instruction to those who have not the assistance of an Oral Teacher. By the aid of this work, any person of the most ordinary intelligence may learn to write Short-Hand, and Report Speeches and Sermons in a short time. Bound in boards, with cloth back. Price..**50 cts.**

Barton's Comic Recitations and Humorous Dialogues. Containing a variety of Comic Recitations in Prose and Poetry, Amusing Dialogues, Burlesque Scenes, Eccentric Orations and Stump Speeches, Humorous Interludes and Laughable Farces. Designed for School Commencements and Amatevr Theatricals. Edited by JEROME BARTON. This is the best collection of Humorous pieces, especially adapted to the parlor stage, that has ever been published. Illuminated paper cover. Price.....**30 cts.**
Bound in boards, with cloth back....................................**50 cts.**

The Secret Out; *or, One Thousand Tricks with Cards, and other Recreations.* Illustrated with over Three Hundred Engravings. A book which explains all the Tricks and Deceptions with Playing Cards ever known, and gives, besides. a great many new ones—the whole being described so carefully, with engravings to illustrate them, that anybody can easily learn how to perform them. This work also contains 240 of the best Tricks in Legerdemain, in addition to the card tricks. 12mo., 400 pages, bound in cloth, with gilt side and back. Price......................**$1 50**

Duncan's Masonic Ritual and Monitor; *or, Guide to the Three Symbolic Degrees of the Ancient York Rite, Entered Apprentice, Fellow Craft, and Master Mason.* And to the Degrees of Mark Master, Past Master, Most Excellent Master, and the Royal Arch. By MALCOM C. DUNCAN. Explained and Interpreted by copious Notes and numerous Engravings. It is not so much the design of the author to gratify the curiosity of the uninitiated, as to furnish a Guide to the Younger Members of the Order, by means of which their progress from grade to grade may be facilitated. It is a well-known fact that comparatively few of the fraternity are "Bright Masons," but with the aid of this invaluable Masonic Companion any Mason can, in a short time, become qualified to take the Chair as Master of a Lodge. Nothing is omitted in it that may tend to impart a full understanding of the principles of Masonry. This is a valuable book for the Fraternity, containing, as it does, the MODERN "WORK" of the order. No Mason should be without it. It is entirely different from any other Masonic book heretofore published.

Bound in cloth. Price.. **$2 50**

Leather tucks (Pocket-book Style), with gilt edges. Price........... **3 00**

"Trumps'" American Hoyle; *or, Gentleman's Hand-book of Games.* Containing clear and complete descriptions of all the Games played in the United States, with the American Rules for playing them; including Whist, Euchre, Bezique, Cribbage, All-Fours, Loo, Poker, Brag, Piquet, Ecarte, Boston, Cassino, Chess, Checkers, Backgammon, Dominoes, Billiards, and a hundred other Games. This work is designed to be an American authority in all games of skill and chance, and will settle any disputed point. It has been prepared with great care by the editor, with the assistance of a number of gentlemen players of skill and ability, and is not a re-hash of English Games, but a live American book, expressly prepared for American readers. THE AMERICAN HOYLE contains 525 pages, is printed on fine white paper, bound in cloth, with beveled boards, and is profusely illustrated with engravings explaining the different Games.

Price.. **$2 00**

Brisbane's Golden Ready Reckoner. Calculated in Dollars and Cents, being a useful Assistant to Traders in buying and selling various commodities, either wholesale or retail, showing at once the amount or value of any number of articles, or quantity of goods, or any merchandise, either by the gallon, quart, pint, ounce, pound, quarter, hundred, yard, foot, inch, bushel, etc., in an easy and plain manner. To which are added Interest Tables, calculated in dollars and cents, for days and for months, at six per cent. and at seven per cent. per annum, alternately; and a great number of other Tables and Rules for calculation never before in print. By WILLIAM D. BRISBANE, A. M., Accountant, Book-keeper, etc.

Bound in boards, cloth back. Price................................ **35 cts.**

The Indian Club Exercise. With explanatory figures and positions, photographed from life; also, general remarks on Physical Culture. Illustrated with portraitures of celebrated athletes, exhibiting great muscular development from the Club Exercise, engraved from photographs. expressly for this work. By Sim. D. Kehoe.

Quarto, cloth. Price... **$2 50**

Live and Learn. A Guide for all who wish to Speak and Write correctly. Containing examples of one thousand mistakes of daily occurrence, in speaking, writing and pronunciation.

216 pages, cloth, small octavo. Price................................ **75 cts.**

Mrs. Crowen's American Lady's Cookery Book. Containing over 1,200 original receipts for preparing and cooking all kinds of dishes. The most popular Cook Book ever published.

12mo., cloth, 474 pages.. **$2 00**

Dr. Valentine's Comic Lectures; *or, Morsels of Mirth for the Melancholy.* A budget of Wit and Humor, and a certain cure for the blues and all other serious complaints. Comprising Comic Lectures on Heads, Faces, Noses, Mouths, Animal Magnetism, etc., with Specimens of Eloquence, Transactions of Learned Societies, Delineations of Eccentric Characters, Comic Songs, etc. By Dr. W. VALENTINE, the favorite Delineator of Eccentric Characters. Illustrated with twelve portraits of Dr. Valentine, in his most celebrated characters.
12mo., cloth, gilt. Price..**$1 25**
Ornamental paper cover. Price..**75 cts.**

The Poet's Companion; *A Dictionary of all Allowable Rhymes in the English Language.* This is a book to aid aspiring genius in the Composition of Rhymes, and in Poetical Effusions generally. It gives the Perfect, the Imperfect, and the Allowable Rhymes, and will enable you to ascertain, to a certainty, whether any words can be mated. It is invaluable to any one who desires to court the muses, and is used by some of the best writers in the country. Price..**25 cts.**

Ladies' Guide to Crochet. By Mrs. ANN S. STEPHENS. Copiously illustrated with original and very choice designs in Crochet, etc., printed in colors, separate from the letter-press, on tinted paper. Also with numerous wood-cuts, printed with the letter-press, explanatory of terms, etc. Bound in extra cloth, gilt. This is by far the best work on the subject of Crochet ever published.
Price..**$1 25**

Chips from Uncle Sam's Jack Knife. Illustrated with over one hundred Comical Engravings, and comprising a collection of over five hundred Laughable Stories, Funny Adventures, Comic Poetry, Queer Conundrums, Terrific Puns, Witty Sayings, Sublime Jokes, and Sentimental Sentences. The whole being a most perfect portfolio for those who love to laugh. Large octavo. Price..**25 cts.**

Fox's Ethiopian Comicalities. Containing Strange Sayings, Eccentric Doings, Burlesque Speeches, Laughable Drolleries, Funny Stories, interspersed with Refined Wit, Broad Humor, and Cutting Sarcasm, copied verbatim, as recited by the celebrated Ethiopian Comedian. With several Comic Illustrations. Price..**12 cts.**

Mind Your Stops. Punctuation made plain, and Composition simplified for Readers, Writers and Talkers. This little book is worth ten times the price asked for it, and will teach accurately in everything, from the diction of a friendly letter to the composition of a learned treatise. Price..**12 cts.**

Hard Words Made Easy. Rules for Pronunciation and Accent; with instructions how to pronounce French, Italian, German, Danish, Dutch, Swedish, Norwegian, and other foreign names. A capital work. Price..**12 cts.**

Bridal Etiquette; A Sensible Guide to the Etiquette and Observances of the Marriage Ceremonies; containing complete directions for Bridal Receptions, and the necessary rules for bridesmaids, groomsmen, sending cards, etc. Price..**12 cts.**

The Universal Book of Songs. Comprising a choice collection of 400 new Sentimental, Scotch, Irish, Ethiopian and Comic Songs. 12mo., cloth, gilt. Price..**$1 25**

How to be Healthy; Being a Complete Guide to Long Life. By a Retired Physician. Price..**12 cts.**

The Finger-post to Public Business. Containing the mode of forming and conducting Societies, Clubs, and other Organized Associations; full Rules of Order for the government of their debates and business; Models of Constitutions, for Lyceums, Institutes, and other Societies. With rules of Cricket, Base-ball, Shinny, Quoits, Yachting and Rowing, and Instructions concerning Incorporations. Hints about Libraries and Museums, with a Catalogue of desirable Books, and a List of American Coins; and Rules for the collection and preservation of books, MSS., and objects of Curiosity. Rules for Debating, and a selection of specimens of style from various American orators. Together with an appendix, containing the original Articles of Confederation of the United States, the Constitution, the celebrated Virginia and Kentucky Resolutions, and other documents of reference. By an Ex-Member of the Philadelphia Bar. 12mo., cloth. Price... $1 50

That's It; *or, Plain Teaching.* By the author of "Inquire Within," "The Reason Why," etc. Illustrated with over 1200 wood-cuts. 12mo., cloth, gilt side and back. This book is a perfect encyclopedia of universal information upon things common and uncommon, found in nature, art and science. The whole visible world is swept within the circuit of its touch, and the subjects are illustrated by wood engravings of an excellent character, done in a high style of that art. It is a library in itself, and to a lad or miss of an inquiring turn of mind, it is a perfect Aladdin's palace of useful and interesting information. Price................. $1 50

The Reason Why: Natural History. By the author of "Inquire Within," "The Biblical Reason Why," etc. This volume answers about 1,500 questions, giving Reasons for hundreds of curious and interesting facts in connection with Natural History, and throwing a light upon the peculiar habits and instincts of the various orders of the Animal Kingdom. More real knowledge can be obtained from this book than from twenty dry works on the same subject.
12mo., cloth, gilt side and back. Price.............................. $1 50

Biblical Reason Why. A Hand-book for Biblical Students, and a Guide to Family Scripture Readings. Beautifully illustrated. Large 12mo., cloth, gilt side and back. This work gives 1,494 Reasons, founded upon the Bible, and assigned by the most eminent Divines and Christian Philosophers, for the great and all-absorbing events recorded in the History of the Bible, the Life of our Saviour and the Acts of his Apostles. Price.. $1 50

The Lady's Manual of Fancy Work. A Complete Instructor in every variety of Ornamental Needle-work, with a list of materials and hints for their selection; advice on making up and trimming. By Mrs. PULLAN, Director of the Work-table of Frank Leslie's Magazine, etc. Illustrated with over 300 engravings, by the best artists, with eight large pattern plates, elegantly printed in colors, on tinted paper. Large octavo, beautifully bound in cloth, with gilt side and back stamp. Price.... $2 00

Harp of a Thousand Strings; *or, Laughter for a Lifetime.* A large book of nearly 400 pages. By the author of Mrs. Partington's Carpet-bag of Fun. Bound in a handsome gilt cover; containing more than a million laughs, and crowded full of funny stories, besides being illustrated with over 200 comical engravings, by Darley, McLennan, Bellew, etc. Price.. $1 50

The Dictionary of Love. Containing a Definition of all the Terms used in Courtship, with rare quotations from Poets of all Nations, together with specimens of curious Model Love Letters, and many other interesting matters appertaining to Love, never before published. 12mo., cloth, gilt side and back. Price............................ $1 50

Martine's Letter-writer and Etiquette Combined. For the USE of Ladies and Gentlemen. 12mo., cloth, gilt side and back. A great many books have been printed on the subject of etiquette and correct behavior in society, but none of them are sufficiently comprehensive and matter-of-fact enough to suit the class of people who may be called new beginners in fashionable life. This book is entirely different from others in that respect. It explains in a plain, common-sense way, precisely how to conduct yourself in every position in society. This book also contains over 300 sensible letters and notes suitable to every occasion in life, and is probably the best treatise on Letter-writing that has ever been printed. It gives easily understood directions, that are brief and to the point. It has some excellent model letters of friendship and business, and its model Love Letters are unequaled. If any lady or gentleman desires to know how to *begin* a love correspondence, this is just the book they want. This volume contains the same matter as "Martine's Hand-book of Etiquette" and "Martine's Sensible Letter-writer," and, in fact, combines those two books bound together in one substantial volume of 373 pages..............$1 50

Horse-taming by a New Method. As Practised by J. S. RAREY. A New and Improved Edition, containing Mr. Rarey's whole Secret of Subduing and Breaking Vicious Horses, together with his improved Plan of Managing Young Colts, and Breaking them to the Saddle, to Harness and the Sulky, with ten Engravings illustrating the process. Every person who keeps a horse should buy this book. It costs but a trifle, and you will positively find it an excellent guide in the management of that noble animal. This is a very handsome book of 64 pages. Price..12 cts.

Knowlson's Farrier, and Complete Horse Doctor. We have printed a new and revised edition of this celebrated book, which contains Knowlson's famous Recipe for the Cure of Spavin, and other new matter. It is positively the best book of the kind ever written. We sell it cheap, because of the immense demand for it. The farmers and horse keepers like it because it gives them plain, common-sense directions how to manage their horses. We sell our new edition (64 pages, 18mo) cheap. Price..12 cts.

The Art of Conversation. With remarks on Fashion and Address. By Mrs. MABERLY. This is the best book on the subject ever published. It contains nothing that is verbose or difficult to understand, but all the instructions and rules for conversation are given in a plain and common-sense manner, so that any one, however dull, can easily comprehend them. 64 pages octavo, large. Price..........................25 cts.

Charley White's Joke Book. Being a perfect Casket of Fun, the first and only work of the kind ever published. Containing a full exposé of all the most laughable Jokes, Witticisms, etc., as told by the celebrated Ethiopian Comedian, CHARLES WHITE. 94 pages. Price..12 cts.

Black Wit and Darkey Conversations. By CHARLES WHITE. Containing a large collection of laughable Anecdotes, Jokes, Stories, Witticisms, and Darkey Conversations. Price..12 cts.

The Nightingale Songster; *or, Lyrics of Love.* Containing 164 Choice Sentimental Songs. Bound in boards, with cloth back, and illustrated cover. Price..50 cts.

The Emerald; *or, Book of Irish Melodies.* Containing a Choice Collection of Irish, Comic, and Sentimental Songs. Bound in boards, cloth back, and illustrated cover. Price..........50 cts.

The Book of 1,000 Comical Stories; *or, Endless Repast of Fun.* A rich banquet for every day in the year, with several courses and a dessert. BILL OF FARE: Comprising Tales of Humor, Laughable Anecdotes, Irresistible Drolleries, Jovial Jokes, Comical Conceits, Puns and Pickings, Quibbles and Queries, Bon Mots and Broadgrins, Oddities, Epigrams, etc. Appropriately Illustrated with 300 Comic Engravings. By the author of "Mrs. Partington's Carpet-bag of Fun."
Large 12mo., cloth. Price..$1 50

Mrs. Partington's Carpet-bag of Fun. A collection of over one thousand of the most Comical Stories, Amusing Adventures, Side-splitting Jokes, Cheek-extending Poetry, Funny Conundrums, QUEER SAYINGS OF MRS. PARTINGTON, Heart-rending Puns, Witty Repartees, etc. The whole illustrated by about 150 comic wood-cuts.
12mo., 300 pages, cloth, gilt. Price..$1 25
Ornamented paper covers..75 cts.

How to Behave; *or, The Spirit of Etiquette.* A Complete Guide to Polite Society, for Ladies and Gentlemen; containing rules for good behavior at the dinner table, in the parlor, and in the street; with important hints on introduction, conversation, etc.
Price..12 cts.

Dr. Valentine's Comic Metamorphoses. Being the second series of Dr. Valentine's Lectures, with Characters, as given by the late Yankee Hill. Embellished with numerous portraits.
Ornamental paper cover. Price..75 cts.
Cloth, gilt..$1 25

Broad Grins of the Laughing Philosopher. Being a Collection of Funny Jokes, Droll Incidents, and Ludicrous pictures. By PICKLE THE YOUNGER. This book is really a good one. It is full of the drollest incidents imaginable, interspersed with good jokes, quaint sayings, and funny pictures. Price..13 cts.

The Knapsack Full of Fun; *or, One Thousand Rations of Laughter.* Illustrated with over 500 comical Engravings, and containing over one thousand Jokes and Funny Stories. By DOESTICKS and other witty writers. Large quarto. Price..30 cts.

The Plate of Chowder; *A Dish for Funny Fellows.* Appropriately illustrated with 100 Comic Engravings. By the author of "Mrs. Partington's Carpet-bag of Fun."
12mo., paper cover. Price..25 cts.

How to Talk and Debate; *or, Fluency of Speech Attained without the Sacrifice of Elegance and Sense.*
Price..12 cts.

How to Dress with Taste. Containing Hints on the harmony of colors, the theory of contrast, the complexion, shape or height.
Price..12 cts.

How to Cut and Contrive Children's Clothes at a Small Cost. With numerous and explanatory engravings. Price..........12 cts.

The Young Housekeeper's Book; *or, How to Have a Good Living upon a Small Income.* Price..12 cts.

The Chairman and Speaker's Guide; *or, Rules for the Orderly Conduct of Public Meetings.* Price..12 cts.

www.ingramcontent.com/pod-product-compliance
Lightning Source LLC
LaVergne TN
LVHW011225110826
845150LV00006B/1549

* 9 7 8 1 4 2 5 5 1 5 2 7 0 *